THE SYMPHONY

1800–1900

A Norton Music Anthology

Also by Paul Henry Lang

MUSIC IN WESTERN CIVILIZATION

MUSIC AND HISTORY

GEORGE FRIDERIC HANDEL

THE EXPERIENCE OF OPERA

A PICTORIAL HISTORY OF MUSIC
(WITH OTTO L. BETTMANN)

PROBLEMS OF MODERN MUSIC (EDITOR)

THE CREATIVE WORLD OF MOZART (EDITOR)

STRAVINSKY: A NEW APPRAISAL OF HIS WORK (EDITOR)

ONE HUNDRED YEARS OF MUSIC IN AMERICA (EDITOR)

THE SYMPHONY, 1800–1900 (EDITOR)

THE CONCERTO, 1800–1900 (EDITOR)

CONTEMPORARY MUSIC IN EUROPE
(EDITOR WITH NATHAN BRODER)

THE SYMPHONY

1800-1900

A Norton Music Anthology

<small>EDITED BY</small>

PAUL HENRY LANG

W · W · NORTON & COMPANY · INC ·
New York

Library of Congress Catalog Card No. 75-77392

ISBN 0 393 02135 1   Cloth Edition
ISBN 0 393 09865 6   Paper Edition

PRINTED IN THE UNITED STATES OF AMERICA

6 7 8 9 0

Contents

Preface

The Symphony in the Nineteenth Century

The selection of the works in this anthology was made not to suit the editor's personal preferences but to permit the student, even within a necessarily limited space, to become acquainted with the mainstream of the symphonic literature of the nineteenth century. This selection was further limited to the purely instrumental symphony, not because symphonies with vocal parts are "impure," but because they are outside that mainstream which it is the purpose of this anthology to illustrate. Similarly, the particular offspring of the symphony, the symphonic poem, was also omitted. We did, however, include Berlioz's *Symphonie fantastique* because it is the most enduring and celebrated of the program symphonies and is to a considerable degree responsible for the secession from the Classical tradition. The program symphony and the symphonic poem deserve a volume of their own, which will eventually be forthcoming.

Needless to say, the symphonies offered here are only samples—but they are representative samples that add up to a nice little library; anything beyond such a selection would be impractical and might even defeat the purpose of this anthology. The reader should bear in mind, however, that the eminent composers appearing on these pages are themselves mere samples—if very superior ones—taken from among a multitude of able composers. There are from the nineteenth century many fine symphonies which, though now forgotten, are entirely viable; perhaps better acquaintance with the masterpieces will lead to a more sympathetic attitude toward the minor masters whose works would afford many hours of thoroughly enjoyable music. There is only one Sunday in the week; but we must also think of the ordinary weekdays that also have their charm and attraction.

For a full discussion of the rise and first development of the symphony the reader is referred to the forthcoming companion volume of eighteenth-century symphonies. Nevertheless, a modicum of repetition is necessary here, even if we proceed with the assumption that the reader is somewhat familiar with the Classical symphony as well as with the underlying sonata principle.

* * *

The home of the symphony was Vienna; yet we should consider the designation "Viennese school" more generic than geographic. Histories of music tend to treat Salzburg, Prague, and Eszterháza as suburbs of Vienna, although they were musical centers removed from the capital and as varied as the ingredients of the Viennese symphony. Among the composers who contributed to the development of the Classical symphony there were a number of non-Germans—Austria was a polyglot empire of Germans, Slavs, Hungarians, and Italians—and what lured them to the capital city was a court and many aristocratic sponsors generous toward music. It would be useful to remark that of all members of the Viennese school, Schubert was the only native son; all the others came from elsewhere. Since among these musicians there were many Czechs who arrived in Vienna as mature and established musicians, "Austro-Bohemian school" would be perhaps a more accurate designation than "Viennese school"; but since the latter term is firmly embedded in musical historiography, and since Vienna became the symbol for the great era that stretches from Johann Josef Fux to Anton Bruckner (and once more from Mahler to Webern), we had better retain the term. While at first, and after a preliminary impulse in Italy, the Classical symphony was indeed created and practiced mainly in Austria, the symphonic idea gradually diffused to the north of Germany, to France, and later to Russia, Finland, and Scandinavia.

As the new century, the nineteenth, opens, all of Europe speaks, or attempts to speak, the language of Vienna. Haydn and Mozart had woven the fabric of music seemingly for eternity. In the Germanic countries the continuation was natural; Haydn was as highly appreciated in Leipzig, Amsterdam, and London as he was in Vienna, and it is indicative of the universal familiarity with the idiom that piratical publishers produced spurious Haydn quartets and symphonies in quantity. As we advance into the nineteenth century we notice that while Viennese Classicism had a strong Latin, notably Italian, vein, the Romantic symphony, especially in the latter part of the period, became almost exclusively German in spirit and tone. Debussy considered Brahms the most German composer of them all. In the Latin countries symphony and quartet remained largely foreign imports. Not that the Classical style was rejected or unknown; it made its appearance in the theater, in church music, and in the conservatory, but it was not practiced as the principal style in instrumental music. To the

Italians and, to a lesser degree, the French, the lyric theater was the very manifestation of life, natural and autochthonous, and most of their composers exerted their energies in working for the opera house and the church, church music having been for a long time closely related to dramatic music. In the century of Romanticism, then, the bulk of the symphonic literature as well as its outstanding representatives will still be German, just as the bulk of the operatic literature and its outstanding representatives will still be Italian. (Wagner is an exception that does not alter the general situation.) To be sure, here and there one finds a distinguished "foreign" master who could speak the Viennese language to perfection, like Cherubini. This mysterious, puritanical conservative, residing in Paris, whom Haydn and Beethoven admired and Berlioz detested, was a true Classic, but he wrote only one symphony; all his magnificent craftsmanship and cool Beethovenian ardor went into the making of operas and large-scale church music. We might also mention an example from the other camp, Saverio Mercadante, called "The Italian Beethoven," whose *Sinfonia fantastica* preceded Berlioz; but he too became famous as an opera composer and left no mark on the history of the symphony.

As the nineteenth century dawned, the symphony, the favorite genre of orchestral music since the latter part of the previous century, had reached such heights as were felt to be unsurpassable. The original mixture of Italian opera derivatives, the German suite, the concerto, the divertimento, and other ingredients had coalesced, mainly under the wise and immensely imaginative Haydn, into a genre and idiom based on the art of development and exploitation of thematic material carried out within a constructive framework that we call the sonata form. The Germans were used to this sort of thing, if in a different medium: fugue and the art of variation; but formerly they operated with themes, whereas the eighteenth-century symphonic procedure favored fractions of themes, mere motifs. A theme has a physiognomy of its own, a motif is only a fragment of a musical idea; a theme is a self-sufficient musical entity, a motif offers only potentialities which can, through elaboration, become the support of a tremendous musical edifice. Perhaps the incarnation of the symphonic ideal, of motivic architecture and logic as well as of overwhelming expressive force, is the first movement of Beethoven's Fifth Symphony; it is built on a little motif of four notes, three of which are repeated. No full-blooded Romantic composer would even look at such an insignificant subject—insignificant in isolation; yet the Classical composers deliberately sought just this sort of material. It did not matter where the original idea came from, as indeed almost all symphonic allegro themes in the eighteenth-century and far into the Beethovenian era came from the public domain; all that mattered was what would happen to it. In this art of elaborating a small particle or snatch of a musical idea, the eighteenth-century composers were infinitely ingenious, the particles assuming all shades of expression, from the humorous to the profound, from the brilliant to the noble. Contrary to the Romantic concept of "invention," which demanded original and unmistakably personal themes, the eighteenth century understood by "invention" the art of elaboration, combination, and permutation of any given subject. Only in opera, and in the slow movements of instrumental works, was melody as an entity preferred; in a symphonic allegro an independent, significant theme would hobble the composer's imagination, because a well-shaped melody cannot be splintered and dissected—such a procedure would ruin it. Motivic-thematic elaboration carries with it a certain melodic frugality. The Classical symphonists were not interested primarily in the sensuous quality of music, but in its possibilities of manipulation; it was not the beauty of the "invention" that mattered to them, but the characteristic melodic-rhythmic profile, the springiness, the many possible "meanings" of the motif in different contexts, the constructive use of the given material. This was the age of witty conversation, the challenge, the quick repartee—and the symphony, played in aristocratic residences rather than in concert halls, conversed with equal wit in the realm of music. The mature eighteenth-century symphony is difficult to grasp, though its elegance and sprightliness always delight and fall easily on the ear, because the incessant sparkle of the thematic convolutions requires the listener's active mental participation. Even today this is difficult to the layman, and it was found difficult by the Romantic composers, too, who eventually had to abandon it and create their own principles of construction and cohesion. The contrapuntal finesse in the late symphonies of Haydn and Mozart, the imitations, the dramatic juxtaposition and opposition of the particles obtained by "exploding" the symphonic subject, are so sophisticated that the more knowledgeable and historically informed composers, like Brahms, hesitated to enter the particular preserves of the Classical composer—i.e., the quartet and symphony.

The formal scheme of the Classical symphonic ideal was the so-called "sonata form," usually associated with the opening allegro, but often appearing in the finale (frequently combined with the rondo) and at times in the slow movement. A good deal of misconception is attached to this constructional scheme, and one frequently encounters the remark that such-and-such a movement is composed in "strict" sonata form. But there was nothing "strict" about the sonata form. In fact, the eighteenth-century composer had not even heard the term, which was coined in the nineteenth century; he followed certain *principles,* not a pattern. The basic concept was to present the idea or ideas to be elaborated in a first section, which our theorists call "exposition," develop this material in the middle or "development" section, then prepare and execute a "recapitulation" or "reprise" in such a manner as to reconcile the warring, antithetic tonalities by restoring the unequivocal supremacy of the main key. Within these general principles the composer was absolutely free; there were no "rules" because the statute books were all written in the nineteenth century, and if Haydn could see them he would have a hearty laugh. Thus, a composer could use a "second" or "subsidiary" theme, or perhaps a whole theme group, but he could also base the entire movement on a single theme. The transition to the subsidiary theme may contain material that later acquires more importance than the principal subject; Haydn often uses a second theme only to ignore it in the elaboration of the exposition—indeed, he may even ignore his principal subject and barrel along magnificently with a little snippet taken from the final cadence in the exposition. This freedom of the sonata form, as opposed to the restrictions we have since read into it, is shown in a variety of ways. For example, the exposition of an allegro movement may present a thematic group we designate ABC, but of this group only A is developed, whereas the reprise ignores A, begins with B, and ends with C; then the coda gives A a generous workout. As a matter of fact, the coda, the postlude in the sonata form, constantly gains in importance. In the last movement of Beethoven's Eighth Symphony, one of his longest movements, and a work in which, as in the Fourth Symphony, he lovingly returns to the eighteenth century, the coda is only a few measures shorter than all the rest of the movement and has a little coda of its own. The overriding principle was not a formal pattern but the logic and continuity of thematic elaboration; whatever was selected for elaboration had to be pursued until all possibilities were exhausted.

There was a certain pattern in the relationship of development to exposition, but even in the eighteenth century it was not binding. Haydn might compose a development section twice the size of the exposition; Mozart might do the same, though he was just as ready to write a large and highly developed exposition and a development that was one third of its size. With Beethoven's Third Symphony (the *Eroica*) and with the Romantic symphonists, the development section expands, though, once more, Schumann and Dvořák were willing to reverse the proportions. Then again, in the second movement of Mendelssohn's Third Symphony ("Scottish") the development is shorter than the exposition and the reprise shorter than the development, but the coda nicely restores symmetry and balance. The exact opposite is true in the fourth movement of Schumann's Second Symphony, where the reprise is almost twice as long as the exposition and the coda twice the size of the reprise. All this goes to show that we should beware of categorical "rules"; they exist only in textbooks written after the fact. To reiterate, the sonata was a "free" rather than a "strict" form, its disposition entirely determined by the composer's will, imagination, and sense of tonal balance; only the principles of thematic development and tonal stress and resolution were binding.

The sonata principle was retained by the "pure" symphony of the nineteenth century, but it was enlarged and extended, often to all four movements. Furthermore, a relationship between the individual movements, the so-called cyclic principle, was established, which may encompass two or even all movements. Simple quotation from preceding movements, however, does not necessarily amount to cyclic construction. The oft-cited example in the finale of Beethoven's Ninth Symphony, where the composer quotes bits from the previous movements, is not of a structural nature; these are only reminiscences that are not organically connected, unlike the case of his Fifth Symphony, where the scherzo and the finale are inseparably entwined. We shall see imaginative and vitally important structural connections between movements in the symphonies of Schumann, Brahms, and Dvořák, and in Bruckner's Eighth Symphony all four movements are united in a mighty contrapuntal apotheosis.

This brings us to an important change in the hierarchy of the movements. In the eighteenth century the first allegro was usually the weightiest movement, but later the finale began to gain in status, to become in Brahms's First and Fourth and in all of Bruckner's symphonies the culmination of the work. The hymnic finale, even in purely instrumental form, is palpably descended from Beethoven's Ninth, though some of his earlier symphonies also contributed to the idea, as the Third, the Fifth, and the Sixth rise to dithyrambic heights in their final movements. The ultimate in the cyclic idea is to be found in Beethoven's last quartets, where the principle transcends the boundaries of the individual work to embrace several of the quartets.

To the eighteenth-century composer, the material dictated not only form and substance, but also their external manifestations, such as the choice and employment of instruments. The Classical composer of symphonies did not orchestrate, he composed for orchestra; that is, the ideas and their realizations came in their full and finished orchestral garb requiring very few adjustments. In his operas Mozart used a far more varied and elaborate orchestral idiom than in his symphonies, and in many a divertimento the winds were given virtuoso tasks that we never encounter in the symphonies. The reason for this was that the terse and dynamic Classical symphony used the weight of the orchestra, especially brasses and drums, not for effect but for delineation of the form and for emphatically nailing down the tonalities. To be sure, there was also color in this orchestra and (especially in Beethoven) many imaginative orchestral turns, but these remained secondary in importance until the late Romantic symphony, and even then were more conspicuous in the French and Russian works than in the German ones.

In the meantime the orchestra underwent considerable change, but since as usual the development took place in the opera pit, the German symphony was unaffected by it, beyond a modest degree, almost to the time of Richard Strauss. The new, "noisy" apparatus, inaugurated by Lesueur, Simon Mayr (an expatriate Bavarian residing in Bergamo), and Gasparo Spontini (an expatriate Italian lording it over Paris, and later Berlin), strongly affected the French, notably Berlioz, as well as Meyerbeer, Liszt, and, to a certain degree, Wagner; but none of these composers was a true symphonist. Perhaps the greatest change influencing the sound of the orchestra in the post-Beethovenian era was the invention of the valves for horn and trumpet. The Classical symphonists, limited to the very restricted number of "natural" tones, tailored their use of these instruments to their capabilities. The horns furnished the glue that bound strings to woodwinds, their octaves, fifths, and thirds gently blending the two choirs; then in the rousing tuttis they united with the trumpets in proclamative assertion. But now both instruments could play all the chromatic tones within their entire compass, inviting a new way of writing for them. (Just the same, it is entirely false and unnecessary to "correct" brass parts in older works, as Mahler and other conductors were wont to do; the eighteenth-century composer knew the limitations and composed accordingly.)

Still, though enlarged to keep pace with the changing style and with the requirements of the larger concert halls, the nineteenth-century German symphony orchestra remained basically unchanged. Beginning with Schumann, the standard Romantic symphony orchestra consisted of pairs of woodwinds, four horns, two trumpets, three trombones, a pair of timpani, and strings, to which Brahms occasionally added a contrabassoon or a bass tuba. Except for the tuba, this orchestra was identical to Beethoven's in the Ninth Symphony half a century earlier. This is surprising if we realize that by the time Brahms composed his First Symphony, Berlioz and Wagner used triple or even quadruple winds, English horn, bass clarinet, up to eight horns, harps, two pairs of timpani, and assorted other percussion. In the symphony, at least in the central European symphony, but also in Tchaikovsky, all this was absent. Dvořák would use the English horn for a solo, and Bruckner raised the number of the horns to eight, but on the whole these were exceptions, and the late Beethovenian orchestra remained the norm. Nevertheless, the use of wind instruments and especially the relationship between the individual choirs underwent some changes, if for no other reason than the liberation of horns and trumpets. The winds still reinforce and articulate, but they also live their own lives. Yet despite the modernized orchestra, the improved wind instruments, and the enriched color scheme, the mainstream of the symphony still, to a large extent, observed the old Classical condition that orchestral effects must not intrude upon the construction. This is what Berlioz no longer understood; but then he no longer composed symphonies in the original sense.

❈   ❈   ❈

Beethoven, who inaugurates the nineteenth century with the Third Symphony that opens our anthology, is the symphonist par excellence; despite his many other great works, his main influence and reputation, his very image is that of the imperious symphonist. Nothing like the *Sinfonia Eroica,* either in size or intensity, had ever before been composed, nor had the world ever before heard such violence in music. The work changed the course of the symphony so suddenly, so thoroughly and irrevocably, that it took all the rest of the century to make peace with it. This tremendous change wrought by Beethoven had its disadvantages too. So taken were the Romantics by the power, dynamism, and expressive qualities of this and the following symphonies that they mistakenly found Haydn childlike and Mozart graceful but without any depth. The *Eroica* has no predecessors; whence it came is a mystery, because even the great sonatas and quartets did not presage such a Promethean step. In his first two symphonies Beethoven stays within traditional limits, but to dismiss these works, as became customary beginning with Berlioz, is nonsense; they are fine pieces and show many traits of the later Beethoven. Indeed, there are direct connections between the Second and Ninth Symphonies.

What stunned—even frightened—was the sheer power emanating from the *Eroica*. Even Goethe was disturbed by the aura of force surrounding Beethoven and did not know how to take this plebeian aristocrat who shoved royalty aside when it got in his way. As was observed by a friend of both Goethe and Beethoven, Bettina Brentano, "In no ruler have I ever seen such consciousness of power." But then this Rhinelander transplanted to Vienna was made of quite different stuff from his contemporaries and successors. He was a total autocrat, both as man and artist; no note was permitted to move on the staves of his scores without his permission and control, whereas the true Romantic is always ready to accede to momentary impulses. This is really the key to the understanding of this man and of his music: conscious and ever-present artistic control over musical matter.

Beethoven's place in the rising Romantic world is difficult to comprehend. Weber died two years before, Schubert one year after him, yet these two are considered full-blooded Romantics. But Beethoven was still a product of the Classical Viennese school, the enhanced subjectivity of his feelings and the vastly increased proportions of his music notwithstanding. He remained a disciple of Haydn, under the aegis of the Classical symphonic ideal—thematic logic to the exclusion of all extraneous material—and while he greatly enlarged the plan of the symphony he also tightened it. What we feel when listening to this music, and what has made him the most universally admired composer, is the very struggle he communicates, the struggle to maintain this disciplined command in the face of the changing artistic world around him. Thus there is a fundamental difference between Beethoven and the true Romantics, to whom the sonata as a formal ideal was occasional, to be deliberately invoked. To Beethoven it was the principle of creation, it was in his soul.

Compared to Mozart, Beethoven was unruly, intemperate, intense, and naked; he could be raw, but his propulsive symphonic force simply carried everything before it, for this was an art the whole world wanted and needed. To immediate posterity all this seemed the incarnation of Romanticism; it was especially the superscriptions over some of his works—the *Eroica*, the *Pastoral Symphony*, the sonata *Les Adieux*, and so forth—that made the new, literary-oriented musical gentry believe that Beethoven was one of their own. They failed to see his unvarying adherence to pure form, musical form, Classical musicality. Yes, he enlarged, overloaded, and almost rent this Classical symphonic form, but he never abandoned the ideal, for it was his mother tongue. He fought with himself, for his own liberty, and superseded himself when he forced upon that mother tongue the new accents of expressivity; he overpowered the musical instruments and maimed the singing voices because, like the North Germans of an earlier time, he saw only the idea and not the means. (Did not Bach make a solo violin play a four-part fugue?) But the Classical sonata concept remained his sole concern. To be sure, it might have only two movements—or seven—and its internal proportions as well as the tonal order did change considerably under his hand, but the basic principles remained intact: only in the last quartets is this objective command relaxed in favor of a more subjective form of communication. When he saw that he could not continue the symphony along the old lines, he abandoned it, as he had earlier abandoned the concerto. There are clear indications that he himself did not consider the choral finale of the Ninth Symphony a satisfactory ending. With him the eighteenth century becomes overcharged and the nineteenth erupts. But Beethoven's is not a Janus face; he carries the Classical symphonic precepts to their summit from which at the same time the decline begins.

The *Eroica* was first performed in 1805. That it was accepted, though found long and difficult, speaks well for the musical literacy of the Viennese elite. The work is difficult even today, both technically and stylistically. In the first printed edition of the score, Beethoven, fully aware of the great stride he had made, gives the following counsel: "This symphony, which exceeds the customary proportions, should preferably be placed shortly after the beginning rather than toward the end of the program, otherwise its effect, the listener being already tired from what took place before, will be diminished." This first symphony in our anthology, which changed the species and laid the nineteenth century wide open to further development, confronts us with the question of extramusical influences on the symphony and their expression in music; it was to be an ever more important problem as the century matured. Beethoven's predecessors were artisan-artists who may have had certain convictions of a political or moral nature, but these seldom appeared in their public life. Now we are seeing a composer who had burning social, moral, and political convictions, which he expressed openly and strongly in his letters and conversations. But did he carry these convictions *directly* into his music?

Everyone knows the story of the dedication of the Third Symphony to the First Consul and of Beethoven's anger at Napoleon's betrayal of the republican cause when he proclaimed himself Emperor. No commentator would omit the story of the composer's impulsive act of tearing off the dedication. But this work is neither a portrait nor does it follow a program; even the subsequent title, "To the memory of a hero," is a mere reference to a certain mood. The symphony perhaps glorifies heroism, but not one note is permitted in it that was not subjected to the most rigorous symphonic logic. Beethoven simply told us about the impressions that prompted the work. This is not program music, nor is even the "Pastoral" Symphony program music, the superscriptions, the chirping birds, and the storm notwithstanding (even its second movement is in a "strict" sonata form, the birds giving us only a sort of extraneous cadenza *after* the form is completed). But everyone in the nineteenth century took these symphonies for program music, both Berlioz and Wagner seeing in them a mandate to abandon pure instrumental forms. This fact, together with the acceptance of the choral finale of the Ninth as a model for the future, not only interfered with a true appreciation of Beethoven, but bedeviled the future course of the symphony.

The perceptive student will notice how inexorably Beethoven's instinct and imagination work even when he is emotionally hard-pressed. In the development section of the first movement of the *Eroica* the conflict becomes more and more acute, the accents, the harmonic and dynamic clashes become sharper, rising to dissonant flaying before the tension suddenly, though reluctantly, subsides. At this point Beethoven does something that is not in the book: he introduces a significant new melody that was not present in the exposition. Furthermore, this new and highly expressive melody is in E minor, a key far distant from the original E♭. His unfailing instinct told him that he must compensate in some manner for the unusually long development by offering a form of diversion that at the same time would permit him to refocus his tonal order, but his sense of coherence never flagged, and the cello line under the "new" theme outlines the movement's first subject. In the recapitulation the new melody is treated as if it had been part of the exposition, so this "innovation," while quite unusual, is altogether within the spirit and even the letter of the Classical symphony. At the recapitulation, the dramatic-symphonic urge is so strong that the second horn cannot contain itself and enters two measures ahead of time while the violins are still sitting on the dominant. This is a magic spot, but it was thoroughly misunderstood throughout the nineteenth century; even Wagner corrected it as a "mistake"!

The scherzo in this symphony is the first of those lightning-fast movements that, as replacements for the minuet, eliminated the last vestiges of courtly or popular dance music in the symphony; every movement now speaks the same language. Beethoven wrote many scherzos before the *Eroica,* but before this particular composition they were joking and jesting in the original meaning of the term, whereas now the music growls and snarls, whispers menacingly only to explode into open threats. This was new and the sole property of its creator. The menacing tone of the Beethovenian symphonic scherzo, its precipitous flight, so unsettled composers that it took Brahms three symphonies before he dared compose a real symphonic scherzo.

✿ ✿ ✿

If Beethoven is a phenomenon difficult to account for in the era that produced musicians like Weber or men of letters like Tieck and Wackenroder, how much more puzzling is the position of Schubert even though he became the symbol of Romanticism in music. He is softer, more intuitive, more sensitive and sensuous than the Classics and less amenable to internal discipline, but at the age of eighteen he is an incomparable master. Schubert matured dangerously early, never finding his true place even though he lived practically all his brief life in his native Vienna, whose sounds and accents he conveyed with a felicity that none of his colleagues in the Viennese school could approach. (Only later, and at a more popular level, did Vienna again produce a musician whose every breath was Viennese: Johann Strauss.) Schubert lived a bohemian life, never knowing where his next meal would come from, and he died so young that his epitaph bewailed an unfulfilled career that left "a rich possession but even fairer hopes." Admittedly, this biographical sketch accords with the generally held view of a Romantic artist's life and sad fate. But popular (and some not-so-popular) historians have failed to look at the music, seeing only a handful from among the hundreds of songs, and the delightful piano pieces, but not the sonatas, chamber music, symphonies, and Masses. For Schubert was Beethoven's spiritual offspring, next to him the greatest instrumental composer of the century, and in turn the spiritual ancestor of Bruckner and a number of other *symphonists.* This gregarious but lonely musician was part and parcel of the great Viennese school of Haydn, Mozart, and Beethoven, though of course at the same time he already belonged to the youthful Romantic movement—therein resides the difference. The hero of *Die Winterreise* is eternally traveling, for the theme is that of passing and departing—a Romantic theme—but between the travels the wanderer rests, and during those rests he dared to stand up to Beethoven, whom he never dared to approach in person. With Schubert there comes the great September of Classicism, a season that Haydn and Beethoven did not know. But September is both summer and fall, and we must beware of ranging Schubert wholly among the Romantics. As an instrumental composer he was a descendant of the Classical school, even if he continued the tradition on his own terms. The dependence on Haydn, Mozart, and Cherubini in the early symphonies is clear; blueprint, orchestration, tone, and manner are altogether within the spirit of the eighteenth century, though the construction is looser and the harmonies are bolder. In the Fourth Symphony, Beethoven intrudes for the first time and the tone becomes a little heavier, though not nearly as much as the title *Tragic Symphony* would suggest. In the following symphonies Schubert returned to the eighteenth century, but both the Eighth and the Ninth are among the supreme creations of the symphonic literature of any period.

The nineteenth century had considerable difficulty in coming to terms with Schubert the symphonist. The trouble was, of course, Beethoven's gigantic shadow, which Schubert could evade, but his contemporaries, his critics, and his public could not. We in the twentieth century should be able to see the true state of affairs, and, indeed, everything will become clear if we grasp the meaning and position of Classicism in the sea of Romanticism.

In spite of the curious antithesis between a bohemian life and such great and disciplined masterpieces as the D minor Quartet, the C major Quintet, and the B minor Symphony (known as the "Unfinished"), Schubert does not show the dualism of early Romanticism in which the dream-like and contemplative is crossed by caprice, passion, and nervousness, qualities that were already in evidence in the *Sturm und Drang* composers led by Carl Philipp Emanuel Bach. One of these early Romantics, Johann Schobert, the emigrant German composer active in Paris who died many years before Schubert was born and who startled the young Mozart, was already a kinsman of Werther, a vacillating, brooding, yet poetic soul open to every mood. Nothing of this sort is displayed in Schubert. And now it becomes clear that the Classical school, the Viennese school, was nothing but an intermezzo, an island in the great stream of Romanticism. On this island sunshine was preferred to moonlight, clear sky to rosy clouds, the whole to the detail, and life to adventure. When after a relatively short separation the two branches of the stream once more united, the Romantic movement could resume its course. Beethoven still bestrides the island but Schubert stands at the confluence; the Classical lessons, strong and abiding, are still there, but Schubert does things that no one before him would have done. He will begin the reprise at the subdominant or the mediant, as indeed he likes to go into the subdominant region for his subsidiary themes too, creating new tonal stresses and colors; in the "Unfinished" the introduction is no longer separated from the exposition; at times (as in the same symphony) the subsidiary themes are almost too beautiful in their warm lyricism, and threaten—but only threaten—to arrest the symphonic procedure. The construction is less stringent than in the Classics and, notably in some of the piano sonatas and the great C major Symphony, Schubert already shows a penchant for the kind of ecstatic enjoyment of certain ideas, lingering over them and endlessly repeating them, that will be the rule with Bruckner. But all this does not matter, for he was a born symphonist who developed ideas with Beethovenian skill and intensity, and every note is unmistakably personal. There are certain spots in his great C major Symphóny (the "Unfinished" did not become known until the 1860s) that few subsequent composers, at any rate the Germans, could forget. The dreamy horn calls that open the last symphony, or the mysterious trombone theme in the middle of its first movement, are echoed in both Schumann's Fourth and Brahms's Second.

Though the magnificent C major Symphony, composed six years after the B minor, is the proud last sentinel of the Classical symphony, the B minor is a more profound and concise work. The first movement is sorrowful, but rises to breathtaking dramatic eloquence, and has a melodic charm of indescribable beauty. Structure and development are exemplary, unmatched by anything that followed in the century. The second movement is one of the most expressive pieces ever composed, and full of original harmonies. This is really the symphony that should have been called the "Tragic," not the innocent Fourth. But now what could follow such transcendental movements? A rousing scherzo, like the one in the C major Symphony that even Beethoven might envy? A romping rondo-finale? Why should this work be burdened with the name "Unfinished"? Did not Beethoven compose a wondrous sonata in F# minor that has only two movements yet is final and complete? It is true that nine orchestrated measures, and extensive sketches, of a projected scherzo are extant, but we can only conjecture about why Schubert abandoned this movement. The work makes a satisfying whole as it stands; let us forget about the title bestowed on this great work and simply call it Symphony in B minor.

* * *

After the Classical episode in the Romantic era, the movement could continue its course save for one tremendous obstacle: Beethoven. The Romantics tried to overcome the obstacle by making him the father of their own art, but fundamentally they did not know what to do with their patrimony. Though they considered it their duty to compose symphonies, their idol's hallmark, their productivity fell off. This was due partly to their dependence on the not-fully-comprehended Beethovenian model and partly to their innate lyric gifts, which were inimical to the symphonic procedure. The symphony had become a much more circumspect affair than before, and most composers were wary in approaching it. Brahms was forty before he ventured into the field, others too took their time, and nine became the fateful number, not exceeded until our time when very minor composers, like Miaskovsky, turn them out in bunches.

The great change the Romantic symphony represents is due to the gradual shift from architectural logic to expressive power. Beethoven achieved this intense expressivity in the *Eroica* but without abandoning architectural logic; and the same is still true to a considerable extent with Schubert. But their successors saw only the expressivity and froze the living architecture into a scholastic pattern, *the* sonata form. Also, being true Romantics, they preferred expressive, songlike themes, which could not be taken apart to be properly developed. Mendelssohn shows this in his "Scottish" Symphony, but his superior musicianship and his devotion to, and knowledge of, the Viennese Classics, turned the attractive, ballad-like theme to good symphonic use. The Classics were parsimonious; they avoided the irrelevant and the additive. When Mozart was upbraided by an aristocratic patron for using "too many notes," his answer was: "Only so many as were needed." The Romantics continually squandered their musical riches; they were effusive and liked to tarry on favored ideas. All of this ran counter to the symphonic ideal.

The generation immediately after the death of Beethoven and Schubert is clearly divided into two groups. One, altogether within the German orbit—Mendelssohn, Schumann, Brahms, Bruckner—wanted to retain the Classical forms; they wrote sonatas, quartets, and symphonies. But while they retained the outlines of the Classical form they filled it with a content that was frequently uncongenial. The composers in the other group, French, or imbued with French culture—Berlioz, Chopin, Liszt—did not write symphonies and chamber music, only an occasional piano sonata, because they did not accept the German heritage. Their field is program music, fantasy, and rhapsody. However, even within the German domain there was a more fantastic Romantic strain that began with Weber, whose symphonies and sonatas avoided both Haydn and Beethoven. Louis Spohr, another good composer though today neglected, shows the hyperchromatic, restlessly modulating tendency of the coming Wagnerian world as early as 1811. And there were others, like Joachim Raff, who wrote program music and used a Gallicized orchestra. (Raff lent a hand to Liszt, whose orchestration needed a little doctoring.) Spohr understood neither Beethoven nor Schubert—indeed, he was repelled by Beethoven; he started from Mozart and Cherubini, but later the dominating influences upon his style came from French and Italian opera. Clearly, our knowledge of the history of the symphony is still scanty; we know the outstanding masterpieces, but not the byways of this history, nor have the influences coming from opera, which were decisive both in the eighteenth and in the nineteenth centuries, yet been examined. It stands to reason that the operatic great of the day—Pacini, Mayr, Meyerbeer—had considerable influence on Berlioz and others. Pacini's outsized orchestra, his extra brass bands offstage were greatly admired and imitated. There was also the continued preoccupation with the finale of the Ninth Symphony, which made the choral finale widely practiced all the way to Liszt and Mahler. And in between, Wagner himself weighs in with a C major Symphony; very Beethovenian and very immature.

❈   ❈   ❈

Mendelssohn was called the "Romantic Classicist," a title justified to the extent that in his symphonies and chamber music he is firmly anchored in the formal and constructive principles of the Classic era. He was a Romantic in mood and sensitivity, but not in craftsmanship, which is of the finest: Classical, elegant, aristocratic, and flexible, with an excellent aptitude for the vanishing art of counterpoint. Mendelssohn's was a happy and harmonious nature. Fantastically precocious, the seventeen-year-old boy amazed the world with the scintillating overture to *A Midusmmer Night's Dream,* but this prodigious start was not followed by a commensurate development. Mendelssohn wrote many more masterpieces —among them fine symphonies, a violin concerto that is one of the prides of the species, and some of the best chamber music of the post-Beethovenian era—but, perhaps because of the hothouse atmosphere in which he was reared by a loving and sheltering family, he failed to go forward. His self-restrained, cordial, and tender but unventuresome nature prevented real struggle and conflict in his music; he had no problems, the music is always beautifully made, crystalline, and melodious, but it does not ascend to the peak of Olympus. He was the last Romantic who could make peace with reality, though at a price; after him there begins the era of eternal conflict, contradiction, and collision.

With the exception of the last movement, there is nothing particularly Italian about this symphony called "Italian." Designated as No. 4, but actually composed nine years before No. 3 (the "Scottish"), it does however convey a sensitive, cultivated, and receptive young man's impressions on beholding the promised land of the arts. Other influences are more palpably present. The third movement is an Austrian minuet, a *Ländler,* while the bugling horns in the trio are an echo of Weber's horn calls from the German forest. The last movement does use some Italian folk material, but the exquisite string writing is that of the *Midsummer Night's Dream* Overture. As we listen to the bracing symphonic rush of the first movement we realize how faithful Mendelssohn remained to his admired symphonic ancestors. While in the famous overture he amazed with his prophetically imaginative and modern orchestration, in this symphony he uses the Classical orchestra in a largely Classical symphonic way—that is, he delineates rather than colors. It is also surprising that this master of the magically flitting scherzo writes an almost "official" minuet in the 1830s! Perhaps it was a form of homesickness. On the other hand, he too was wary of the Beethovenian model. His scherzos are as swift as Beethoven's, but they are delectable fairy music; not a trace do they show of the menacing quality that made a little boy sitting next to Schumann at a performance of Beethoven's Fifth Symphony cuddle up to him and say "I am afraid."

This is a fine symphony, a delight to the ear, and only the grim and unsmiling anti-Romanticists of a few decades back could sneer at this gentle, refined, and accomplished composer. The weakness in Mendelssohn's music was the very thing that assured its early triumph: its easy flow and undisturbed, mellifluous continuity. His unwavering faith in pure forms instilled in him a great reverence for the past, and he was the first conductor to show interest in the music of the past, *vide* his celebrated revival of Bach's *St. Matthew Passion.* Whatever his detractors have said about him, Mendelssohn was dearly loved and respected by Schumann, Brahms, Dvořák, and Bruckner, and no Romantic in the nineteenth century escaped his influence. We must also remember that this was the time, the late 1830s, when the trivial literature of showpieces that characterized later mass musical culture took its beginning; this noble musician guarded against it, wanting to save what could be saved. It was especially this that endeared him to the crusading critic-editor-composer whose Fourth Symphony is our next item.

❋ ❋ ❋

Robert Schumann was the exact opposite of Mendelssohn. The univer-

sity student of the 1830s, enthusiastic, thirsting, wild, and passionate, remained the eternally youthful student who, far from reconciling his
conflicts with the external world, always managed to find new thorns.
Though cultivated and well-read, Schumann was also naïve and surpris-
ingly lacking in any historical sense, a condition that inhibited not only
the critic but also the composer. The symphony he did not really understand—there is his famous judgment of Mozart's G minor Symphony in
which he saw only "lightness and grace"—yet he composed most attractive
music for his symphonies in which he constantly atones for the weaknesses.
Being primarily a keyboard composer (though also a fine song writer), his
imagination was pianistic; his ideas did not come to him in orchestral
garb, they had to be adapted to the medium. This created an entirely new
situation never before known to symphonists, and today's conductor must
possess solid musicianship and orchestral *savoir-faire* to guard against
awkward balances and cloudy spots. Schumann's intentions were laudably
symphonic. The introduction to the first movement of the Fourth breathes
the spirit of the profound preambles of Haydn, and the theme of the
Allegro is seldom lost sight of; this theme, though spirited, is not a good
symphonic theme, being obviously a pianistic idea. The music is engaging
nonetheless, especially the delightful subsidiary theme, and whenever
Schumann blunders into a blind alley, which is not infrequent, he uses
this fine melody to good advantage and we are immediately ready to
forgive him. The picture changes constantly as Schumann jumps from one
idea to the other, at times within eight or even four measures, once more
compelling the conductor to adroit manipulation of tempo and dynamics.
The new piano style that dominated Schumann's imagination was full of
nervousness and played with ideas and colors in a loose manner, but it was
also like a sensitive kaleidoscope and often highly poetic. This musical
language is not suited to the symphony; it favors a fantasia-like form, an
improvisatory style, its images created by the free association of ideas.
This pianistic thinking created a new role for the accompanying instru-
ment in Schumann's great songs, and the piano fairly dominates in his
mixed chamber music, while in his concerto the participation of the orchestra is more tolerated than encouraged.

The Fourth is really Schumann's second symphony, performed as such
in 1841, but revised and reorchestrated in 1853. Here Schumann endeav-
ored to create more than a cyclic construction; he wanted the work so
unified that even the pauses between the movements were eliminated. We
must bear in mind, however, that the original title of the Fourth Symphony

was *Introduction, Allegro, Romanza, Scherzo, and Finale in one movement;* thus we can see that Schumann had actually in mind a fantasia-like composition, as in his piano concerto, rather than a *bona fide* symphony. The cyclic connections are real: for instance, the principal idea in the Introduction reappears as a subsidiary theme in the Romanza, while elements of the Allegro return in the Finale. In his later years Schumann was affected by a form of rhythmic paralysis, an inability to break out of a pattern, which became a mannerism, unfortunately present in this symphony, especially in the last movement. It is once more his fine lyric invention that brings relief to the monotony of rhythm and meter.

❋ ❋ ❋

While thoroughly Romantic in his concepts, Schumann always defended "absolute" music and in his later years even removed the fancy titles from some of his piano pieces. Not so the composers who next demand our attention. The French, always starting from literary premises, were particularly fond of programs, Grétry even seriously suggesting that Haydn's symphonies should be equipped with texts. It is against this background that we must examine Hector Berlioz and the program symphony.

The program symphony was by no means a novelty, as indeed program music in one form or another had existed since classical antiquity, but for our purposes it should suffice to say that such examples as Dittersdorf's symphonies on Ovid's *Metamorphoses* were well known and liked, and many of Haydn's symphonies acquired nicknames, "The Clock," "The Philosopher," and so forth. Most of this, however, was an innocent game and did not affect structural values, and in the Haydn symphonies one would be hard put to find any connection between their content and their names. The many delightful jokes and surprises in Haydn's symphonies are *musical* jokes and have no conceptual meaning. He may fool us with a false recapitulation only to take us on another thematic rampage, or he may insert unexpected pauses, double or halve the note values, etc., all of which makes us smile—but the tickle is a purely musical tickle and the smile expresses delight in musical inventiveness. If the listener so desires, he can freely apply his own mental associations, as the French did when they gave Haydn's symphonies their pleasant sobriquets; but that is his affair, not the composer's. The essential difference between the symphonists who followed the eighteenth-century ideal and those who espoused the trend begun by Berlioz and Liszt was that the former never permitted the inner logic of the music to be disturbed by any other consideration. The original impetus may have been altogether extramusical—

a storm, a sunrise, personal bereavement—and the composer might be deeply affected by it, but the musical realization of these impressions was in exclusively musical terms. When asked about the finale of his "Romantic" Symphony (No. 4), which is supposed to depict the romanticism of medieval chivalry, Bruckner, with his honest simplicity, answered that he could no longer recall what he had in mind when he composed it. But with Berlioz we find an altogether different concept. The scores of Lesueur, his teacher, are filled with written instructions, veritable itineraries to be followed by the music, thus determining the course of the composition by extramusical, verbal directions. The "vain game" with absolute forms did not interest these Frenchmen; a hundred years before Berlioz, Fontenelle exclaimed in disgust: "Sonata, leave me alone!" Music in itself is not enough, they said; it should be associated with and led by literature. This attitude of course flies into the face of the symphonic ideal, and while Berlioz enthusiastically accepted and practiced this literature-begotten symphony, he could not altogether ignore the basic constructional features of the genre and therefore could not avoid grave discords and discrepancies.

Berlioz did not hail from Eastern Europe, like Chopin or Liszt; he came from the land that can boast the oldest musical culture in the West, and yet he had few ancestors and no artistic progeny. He stands alone because he approached music from without, and often violently. Having abandoned medicine, he threw himself into music, beginning his studies with the bewildering combination of Gluck and Lesueur. To the end of his life he remained essentially a self-made composer; even his extraordinary ability in handling the orchestra was mastered step by step, experimentally rather than organically. He did not know much music, and what he knew he misunderstood. Bach completely escaped him, Mozart he found "boring," Haydn he judged to be a composer for children, and Rossini he dismissed as a detestable rascal. Even Liszt, his friend and unselfish supporter, who made the piano reduction of the *Symphonie fantastique* and thereby helped to disseminate it, he called a "bungler." He does not seem to have paid any attention to the fine if small French school of symphonists on the periphery of the Classical school—Gossec, Méhul, Cherubini—of which both Beethoven and Schubert were admirers. (Incidentally, there was a definite French influence on the German symphonists in the early part of the nineteenth century, if perhaps more from opera than from the symphony, that has not yet been fully explored.) The contradictions in Berlioz's acts and aims were as baffling as those in his music. He worshipped Gluck, but in his own works contradicted him; Weber he hailed as a brother, but mangled the score of *Der Freischütz* almost beyond recognition; he said that the idea for the *Symphonie fantastique* was conceived after reading Goethe's *Faust,* but aside from the *Walpurgisnacht* (Witches' Sabbath) not the faintest connection can be found. Berlioz proudly called himself Beethoven's continuator, but replaced the German symphonic architecture based on tonal stress and concordance and thematic development by a unity created with the aid of a leitmotif, the *idée fixe.*

Actually, what Berlioz attempted in his symphonies was to make the Beethovenian model more understandable by associating the musical proceedings with a conceptual "script." But this was a contradiction in terms, for the essence of the Beethovenian symphony—of the symphonic ideal itself—is purely musical and cannot be verbalized. Berlioz could manipulate a whole musical idea very effectively—witness the metamorphoses of the *idée fixe*—but to take a symphonic subject apart and carry the thematic splinters through rain and shine, as the great symphonists before and after him did, was not within his powers. In addition, his harmonic sense was not equal to the long-range tonal planning a symphonic movement demands. The "episodes from the life of an artist" that this symphony purports to present are indeed episodes within a vague symphonic framework. The *idée fixe* did offer a musical unity, but it was a cognitive rather than a symphonic unity. Berlioz' sonata constructions are the least successful movements in his symphonies, for he invariably gets himself entangled in situations from which he must extricate himself. The escape is often rather primitive, as in the first movement of the *Fantastique,* where early in the game he races up and down the chromatic scale until he makes renewed thematic contact. At other times, however, he saves himself by veritable strokes of genius, though not always of a symphonic nature.

The inner laws of musical symmetry and logic no longer concerned Berlioz, nor did the traditional formal precepts. The ball scene in the *Fantastic Symphony* is not the formerly obligatory minuet or scherzo, it is determined by the story; it is scenic, a picture, a spectacle. As for the internal mechanism of music, Berlioz can be disconcertingly awkward. It was this, more than the idea of the program symphony, that repelled many other musicians. That fastidious craftsman, Mendelssohn, found Berlioz's scores "dirty," and Schumann, though valiantly defending the Frenchman, later shared Mendelssohn's aversions. But Berlioz was a dedicated composer who deeply believed in what he was doing; with his ardor and imagination he could breathe life even into musically weak compositions, and even the weak works have their fine moments. And when he does not follow the Beethovenian model but strikes out into his own fantastic world, as in the last movements of this symphony, he is highly original and convincing.

Berlioz not only enlarged the orchestra by increasing the number of wind instruments and percussion, he also added instruments heretofore absent from the symphony. This orchestra he manipulated with endless imagination, frequently dividing not only violins and violas but the entire string body including the double basses. With that brilliant orchestra, his verve, and his rhythmic vitality, he can carry the day, whatever his other shortcomings may be—which is why he is such a favorite with laymen. These orchestral effects are shrewdly calculated and often bear no relation to the musical idea, but in his later works they are just as often the result of poetic imagination.

The gigantic proportion, the overflowing passion, the colossal apparatus, and the all-encompassing eloquence of Berlioz's dream were half hidden by his aggressive, bilious, and excitable manner, his malicious hysteria, and his sensation-seeking acts and poses. His fate was to be the first musician-victim of the metropolis, lost in the labyrinth of politics, press, and vested interests. He tried to play the appropriate role, but he did not really understand the cruel game and was always the loser. Unquestionably, he did not fully exploit his considerable talents, permitting the grandiose gestures to get the upper hand, but in works like the *Queen Mab Scherzo* and in many stretches in *L'Enfance du Christ*—all quiet and intimate music!—he showed how far these talents could reach when not misdirected or pre-empted by extramusical conditioning and calculation for effect. Perhaps it was Daumier, that perceptive painter, who saw most clearly the character of this great untamed musician when in his portrait he presented Berlioz as the black demon of the storm.

The program symphony and the symphonic poem represent in orchestral music the movement long since apparent in piano music: the turning away from the Haydn-Beethoven type of idiom and construction. Berlioz, Liszt, and others of this persuasion wanted to place expression and representation in the foreground and this at the expense of what they considered the constricting confines of the sonata-symphony. To arrive at a characteristic and graphically explicit representation they relied on elements such as sound effects, harmonic and dynamic eccentricities out of context, and so forth, which were detrimental to symphonic thought. They now saw music under two aspects: as an art, but also as a direct expression of the realities of life and nature. The *Symphonie fantastique* was followed by Liszt's two symphonies, but—significantly—Liszt called the three movements of his *Eine Faust Symphonie* "character pictures."

❖   ❖   ❖

Around 1860—that is, at the time when Liszt and Wagner were reaching the summit—there were signs indicating that the Romantic synthesis was not valid for the ages, that it was beginning to crumble. It became evident that the program symphony had created a crisis threatening to engulf the "absolute" symphony, and that either of the two had enough vitality to lead an independent life. The pure symphony returned to the Classical precepts, hoping for rejuvenation, but was not capable of starting an altogether new life, like its adversary, the program symphony. Instead it turned into a classicistic late Romanticism filled with nostalgic resignation. In Brahms and Bruckner we see the end results of this movement to return to Beethoven and Schubert, but they were preceded by a steady line of composers, now forgotten, who followed in Mendelssohn's wake. Among these symphonies there are a number of works that are still viable and would be enjoyed by modern audiences—if the conductors only knew them.

When Schumann died, Liszt was working on his *Faust Symphony* and Wagner was beginning to sketch *Tristan und Isolde*. These two were the great coryphaei of contemporary German music, yet Schumann considered neither of them his rightful successor; he saw his ideals continued by the young Brahms, whom he had recently discovered. This shows that in his mind there had already begun the estrangement of the two branches of Romanticism, the conservative and the revolutionary. Our path must needs follow the former, because it was among the conservatives that the purely instrumental symphony, the programless symphony, continued its evolution. Now at its noon, the movement had to take a crucial turn. Having lost its youthful and naïve ardor, this Romanticism takes leave of its hopes and illusions, of its innocent faith; henceforth it will eternally pine for this lost innocence. Its other branch, the revolutionaries, struck a different tone; they became determined and aggressive, drunk with the awareness of their individuality, and as Wagner writes to one of his friends: "The natural condition of my soul is ecstasy; I am my own self only when I am beside myself." It was in this split Romantic world, in 1876, that a new master of the old symphony appeared.

❖   ❖   ❖

At the age of twenty, Johannes Brahms turned away from Liszt's circle in Weimar, joining Schumann's musical household, where he was warmly received. Now the young musician had to prove himself both to his detractors and to his friends, who, after Schumann's enthusiastic announcement of the arrival of a composer of unlimited promise, expected great deeds from him. Was it this, the constantly felt need for justification, that developed in him a severe discipline and self-examination and an ever-deepening melancholy? Or was it distaste for and reaction to the sensation-seeking, even demagogic, climate of neo-Romanticism that isolated him in retreat in Vienna, where this North German chose to spend all his mature life? Of great importance to his future was a brief employment as choirmaster in Detmold, where he immersed himself in the study of Renaissance and Baroque music, acquiring a remarkable knowledge, a critical knowledge, of a musical literature known to few in those days. He was always afterwards browsing in old scores, collecting manuscripts, and befriending the first generation of modern musicologists.

This comprehensive knowledge of music, the intimate acquaintance with the great masters of the past, also had its dangers—it could act as a brake. What was once a living and creative force could easily turn into academicism, mere Classical learning. We see the reappearance of long-forgotten rhythmic patterns, the simple tone of old suite music, the strophic song, the elaborate contrapuntal art of his North German ancestors, though also the adventurous harmonies of Schubert. His whole being was saturated with this Indian summer: the past, always the past, the revered masters, Bach, Handel, Mozart, Haydn, Beethoven, Schubert, and the more recent heroes, Mendelssohn and Schumann. As the old masters' metric, rhythmic, and formal qualities are revived in Brahms's music, he abandons in his sonata constructions the open melodies of the Romantics to return to the *ars combinatoria,* the old art of manipulating small motifs. Even his orchestra, whose machinery he slowly mastered in serenade and variation before attempting a symphony, becomes more and more archaic in sound and manner; it too is autumnal, northern, organlike. His filigree work is outstanding but dense and complicated, giving the impression of a certain self-consciousness, and the form is in half light. All of this was ruthlessly attacked by the Wagner party, but by the end of the century Brahms had triumphed, because his was a beautiful and honest struggle that produced great art. Brahms was a Romantic in that he yielded to changing moods and feelings, but he was altogether devoted to Classical logic of construction and procedure and, like his great spiritual mentor,

Beethoven, was also an incomparable master of the art of variation. He saw the "absolute" quality in Beethoven's music and never took his eyes from him. Hugo Wolf, his sworn enemy, remarked that "Brahms writes symphonies as if nothing had happened since Beethoven," but it is precisely this faithfulness to the Classic symphonic ideal that places Brahms in the mainstream of the history of the symphony, while Berlioz remains an exotic if interesting sport.

Brahms's orchestra is altogether in the service of this ideal, for nowhere does he extend the *function* of the symphonic orchestra as did his contemporaries. Judging from his scores, one would think that he had never heard of Berlioz, Liszt, and Wagner; yet he knew the other camp well, and he also knew and greatly admired the piquant orchestra of Bizet, but he could not be deflected from his own way.

The dualism in Brahms's soul, the worship of the past and the delight in the beauties of the Romantic present, is expressed in the differing physiognomy of his symphonies. The great E minor Symphony (No. 4) glories in the past; with its prevailingly dark colors it is a great autumnal threnody. But the symphony in this anthology, the F major, supports the present; Hans Richter, its first conductor, called it Brahms's *Eroica*. Composed in 1883—Brahms was then fifty—it is the shortest of the four, more condensed and plastic as well as more personal than its sisters. How thoroughly Brahms understood and shared the Classical concept of the symphony is best demonstrated in the choice of his material. He uses a motto or, considering his North German origin, perhaps a secret cantus firmus. In the First Symphony he uses the simplest of motifs, C-C♯-D; in the Second the motto is even simpler, D-C♯-D, yet it too dominates in a hundred disguises; now in the Third Symphony we have F-A♭-F, a more pregnant melodic step with a heroic tinge. The procedure followed is interesting: what appears to us as the main subject is really a counterpoint set against the motto. In the development Brahms follows an eighteenth-century practice; it is brief and pays relatively little attention to the main subject, which is left to the coda to be dealt with. Form and thematic material are closely interlocked, and only repeated hearings will disclose the sophisticated construction in this freely flowing movement.

As is so often the case in the eighteenth-century symphony, and even in Beethoven, the slow movement silences trumpets, trombones, and drums. In the present symphony, both inner movements are in this more intimate mood. Brahms did not venture a true symphonic scherzo until his last symphony; the Beethovenian model was too forbidding. Thus the third movement is not a scherzo but a more relaxed piece. The last movement labors under a strong inner stress—as early as in the main subject, there is a major-minor conflict. The cyclic connections are strong, and in the coda of the finale the motto of the first movement returns to round out the form.

✿　✿　✿

Before turning to Bruckner, the last in the line of conservative Romantic symphonists, we must take a look at the so-called national schools. Though this may appear as an excursion into foreign parts, it soon becomes clear that the composers belonging to these national schools are more or less closely related to the Viennese heartland of the symphony; for whether Slavs or Scandinavians, they all were musical pupils of Central Europe. It is from the Germans that they learned the grammar, syntax, and idiom of the symphony; and while at first they merely copied the language, eventually they accommodated it to their own accents. Characteristically, when they did learn the Western musical technique, they could see only with Western eyes even in their own home, like the countryman in the city. No matter how Czech Dvořák's music is, how Russian Tchaikovsky's, it is European music, whereas Mussorgsky is far more Russian than European. To possess validity in the West, this Eastern national music had to satisfy one of two conditions: either to please as ethnic exoticism, or to be "like our own." However, if it satisfied the latter, it had to be on a par with Western art. The success of a Dvořák or a Tchaikovsky was due to their ability to satisfy not one but both of these requirements, especially the second, in ample measure.

According to a popular proverb, every Prussian is born with a sword and every Czech with a French horn. Burney called Bohemia "the conservatory of Europe," because especially since the early eighteenth century that country has produced a host of accomplished musicians, and her contribution to the Viennese school was substantial. Since Bohemia was for hundreds of years a Habsburg crown land, and the Czechs were Austrian subjects, there was a lively coming and going between Prague and Vienna and between the respective provinces. But Czechs also contributed most of the leaders to the Mannheim school too. The influence of the great Austrian masters was understandably strong, and such early Czech Romantics as Tomášek or Kalliwoda, very popular not only in their homeland but also all over Germany, are almost entirely part of the Central European hegemony. What we call the Bohemian national school began in the second half of the nineteenth century. Its father was Bedřich

Smetana, who shows a close affinity with the rich folk art of his country. However, because Smetana was particularly interested in one-movement symphonic poems and in opera, where the national colors showed to better advantage than in the traditional symphony, our first genuine Czech national Romantic symphonist is Antonín Dvořák.

Dvořák followed in Smetana's footsteps with his popular *Slavonic Dances,* but he was also deeply imbued with the art of the Classic and Romantic symphonists and familiar with contemporary trends in the West. The basic influence on his music came from Beethoven and Schubert, then from Mendelssohn and Brahms, but soon Bohemian national elements claimed attention, and also a modicum of Wagner. The folk elements are perceived by us in accents characteristic of Bohemian dances, for like Bartók, Dvořák seldom quotes directly, rather infusing his compositions with the spirit of national music. Though altogether beholden to the German symphonic tradition, and lovingly weighing the art of his great contemporary Brahms, Dvořák is everywhere original and always faithful to his national heritage. He is disciplined, a true symphonist, but can also be capricious and unpredictable.

The numbering of Dvořák's symphonies is a little confusing. All told, he composed nine—again the fateful number—but the first four were originally unnumbered, while the last five, though numbered, were not listed in chronological order. In this country he is best known for his last, American-born symphony, the "New World." But the Eighth, offered here, fascinates with its rather unusual freedom of construction. One is impressed by Dvořák's ability to unite disparate elements into a convincing whole. The first movement, very Romantic with its elegiac introduction, has a plethora of themes held together loosely but imaginatively; then in the midst of this tumble of themes the slow introduction returns, creating a hushed quiet. The second movement, quite personal and original, once more unites various moods, as if Dvořák is reminiscing of his youth, of the church services and the outdoor festivities. The third is the most Slavic of the four movements, reminding one of Tchaikovsky's finer short movements except that the morbid, which with the Russian usually lurks in the background, is altogether missing in this healthy and earthy musician. The finale, a set of variations, is also a potpourri of folk dances and melodies, but the theme is really a paraphrase of the principal theme of the first movement, and thus the merriment hides a cyclic construction.

✿ ✿ ✿

Then as now a forbidden land, only a portion of which belongs to

Europe (and that portion hermetically sealed from the West), Russia made contact with the European symphony at the height of the Romantic movement. Add to this the mistrust of the West and the xenophobia that is always part of the Russian character, and we are faced with a quaint situation. In literature the Russians were mainly French-oriented, and French was the intelligentsia's second language; therefore it is natural that French music attracted them. Furthermore, the colorful French orchestral idiom ideally suited the pseudo-orientalism of fashionable Russian music as exemplified in Rimsky-Korsakov. Other Russian composers, however, frowned on such things, wanting to be Russians without the Western veneer, and there arose, therefore, two schools: the Russophiles, disdaining foreign entanglements, and those who wanted to join the outside world. A particular feature of Russian music of the Romantic era was the predominance of amateur composers. Coming from the military or the professions, guards officers, and engineers composed but seldom finished their works. So it happened that the greatest and most original Russian genius of the century, Mussorgsky, remained an untutored composer to the end of his life; his tremendous opera, *Boris Godunov*, is hardly ever heard in its original form, either in Russia or the West, because it has been repeatedly patched up by professionals. Under these circumstances, it is not surprising that the one full-fledged professional who gained enthusiastic acceptance the world over came from the ranks of the Western-oriented composers.

Mussorgsky both stayed away from Western symphonic thought and denounced it, but Tchaikovsky, while thoroughly Russian in spirit and often in his themes, worked hard at acquiring it. It was not an easy task, for the natural Russian bent is for repetition, not development, and the Russians liked as subjects well-shaped melodies that did not lend themselves to symphonic elaboration, while their orchestral taste ran to the coloristic rather than to·the constructional. Nevertheless, this highly endowed musician managed to overcome these obstacles as did no other Russian in his century. It must be understood, of course, that this altogether personal achievement was entirely within the late Romantic concept of the symphony, for like most Russians, Tchaikovsky knew and appreciated only a very small portion of the Western literature of music. He adored Mozart, possibly because the latter's music was the absolute antithesis to the Russian psyche, but all he could see in the *Well-Tempered Clavier* was finger exercises. Tchaikovsky was a master of the orchestra, with an ability ranging from exquisite needle point to blatantly vulgar tuttis. In fact, his use of the power of the orchestra for ecstatic-hysterical pounding established a new model for mass effects greatly relished in the early part of our century and still popular with concert audiences.

This music, full of verve, bathed in Bengal light, and overflowing with Slavic gloom and sentimentality, was conceived somewhere between ball-room and garret. With its characteristically *fin-de-siècle* quality it represents on the one hand the triumph of the West in Russia, on the other, fashionable Slavic Romanticism in the West.

If we speak of the "expressive symphony," the Fourth of Tchaikovsky's six symphonies is the epitome, although it also shows qualities that go back to the finest traditions of the West. The treatment of the orchestra is so idiomatic that it influences the invention. Tchaikovsky himself stated that the scherzo was born of the pizzicato sound of the strings, while the trio is altogether based on woodwind sonorities. The symphony is cyclic, as the introduction furnishes material for multiple use, and the first three movements are nicely shaped. But the last is perplexing—although it quotes some fine Russian tunes, it has no recognizable shape or even procedure; all of it is mood music, here melancholy and depressed, there thrashing blindly, with cymbals and big drum rending the air.

It is curious that this well-made, splenetic, rich, and overflowing music was composed by a defenseless, frightened, and hesitating man. He was very Russian in his vacillation between the extremes of total resignation and passion verging on brutality. His fortissimo pathos, the great crescendos constantly aiming at frenetic climaxes, was greatly appreciated until anti-Romantic taste rejected him as being obvious and trying, and during the last decade or two it became fashionable among younger musicians to dismiss Tchaikovsky contemptuously as an insufferable vulgarian. But this Russian cannot be peremptorily dismissed. While daily communing with his music is not advisable, he deserves to a considerable extent the popularity that was once his, and he cannot be missing from the history of the Romantic symphony.

❊   ❊   ❊

Like Brahms, Anton Bruckner was a prisoner of the past, and like Brahms, Beethoven and Schubert were his principal ancestors. Inept in artistic politics—as was Brahms—he let himself be maneuvered into the unpleasant position of figurehead in the anti-Brahms party and considered as the Wagnerian representative in the world of the symphony. Yet while his admiration for the Lord of Bayreuth was boundless, he was not really a Wagnerian, all the brassy bugling notwithstanding; by the time of his Seventh Symphony, whose great Adagio is included here, he was much closer to Brahms than to Wagner. Their common ancestry made this inevitable.

Bruckner presents difficulties for non-German audiences and musicians. The combination of a deep religiosity with a naïvely amazed contemplation of nature made him a Baroque mystic in the midst of the Romantics. At the same time he was as Austrian as Schubert. That he could not leave the scene, so to speak, of a church service, or the Vienna forest, or a peasant dance without lovingly lingering over its flavor led to shortcomings in his symphonies, for the kind of symphony he had in mind, the Beethovenian, does not approve of tarrying. With Bruckner the structure widens enormously. He picks up Schubert's predilection for enlarging themes to theme groups, and in addition inserts episodes that likewise grow into groups of episodes—all of which must be developed, resulting in vastly enlarged proportions. (It was this very fact that compelled us to restrict ourselves to one movement of a Bruckner symphony; a whole work would have occupied a disproportionate space in the anthology.)

There is a certain orthodoxy in Bruckner: he always composes the standard four-movement symphony and he observes an unchanging academic order in each of them; all symphonies begin softly and gradually build to more powerful sounds; he favors one type for each movement— for instance, all his scherzos are alike, earthy, rustic, Austrian; the slow movements are compound pieces over which floats the memory of the great slow movement from Beethoven's Ninth Symphony. His orchestra— when not tampered with by editors and conductors—sounds like the organ he played and loved all his life.

There is no denying that frequently the listener's staying power is severely tried. It seems that, unlike Brahms, Bruckner did not grasp the essence of form and keeps weaving for the sake of weaving, creating noble, moving, sincere, but overdimensioned music. In his letters there are sentences that contain seventy or eighty words, clauses and subclauses, so that only repeated reading will disclose the connections. So too, the symphonies require repeated hearings before we can fit everything in its proper place. This is a very difficult and very particular style for us to absorb, but Bruckner repays the labor such an understanding demands. He was a childlike, innocent, guileless, and deeply religious man who thought that by placing tower upon tower he would get closer to the "good Lord" to whom he dedicated his last symphony. In his work, there ends the long history of the German symphony—ends, depending upon who is looking at it, in glory or in dissolution. At any rate, and whatever our beliefs, we have arrived at the crossroads; what follows no longer belongs in this volume.

THE SYMPHONY

1800–1900

A Norton Music Anthology

Ludwig van Beethoven *(1770–1827)*

SYMPHONY NO. 3 IN E♭ MAJOR,

OP. 55 ("EROICA")

(1 8 0 3)

INSTRUMENTATION

2 Flutes
2 Oboes
2 Clarinets in B♮
2 Bassoons

3 Horns in E♮, C, F
2 Trumpets in E♮, C

Timpani

Violin I
Violin II
Viola
Cello
Double Bass

I

129

136

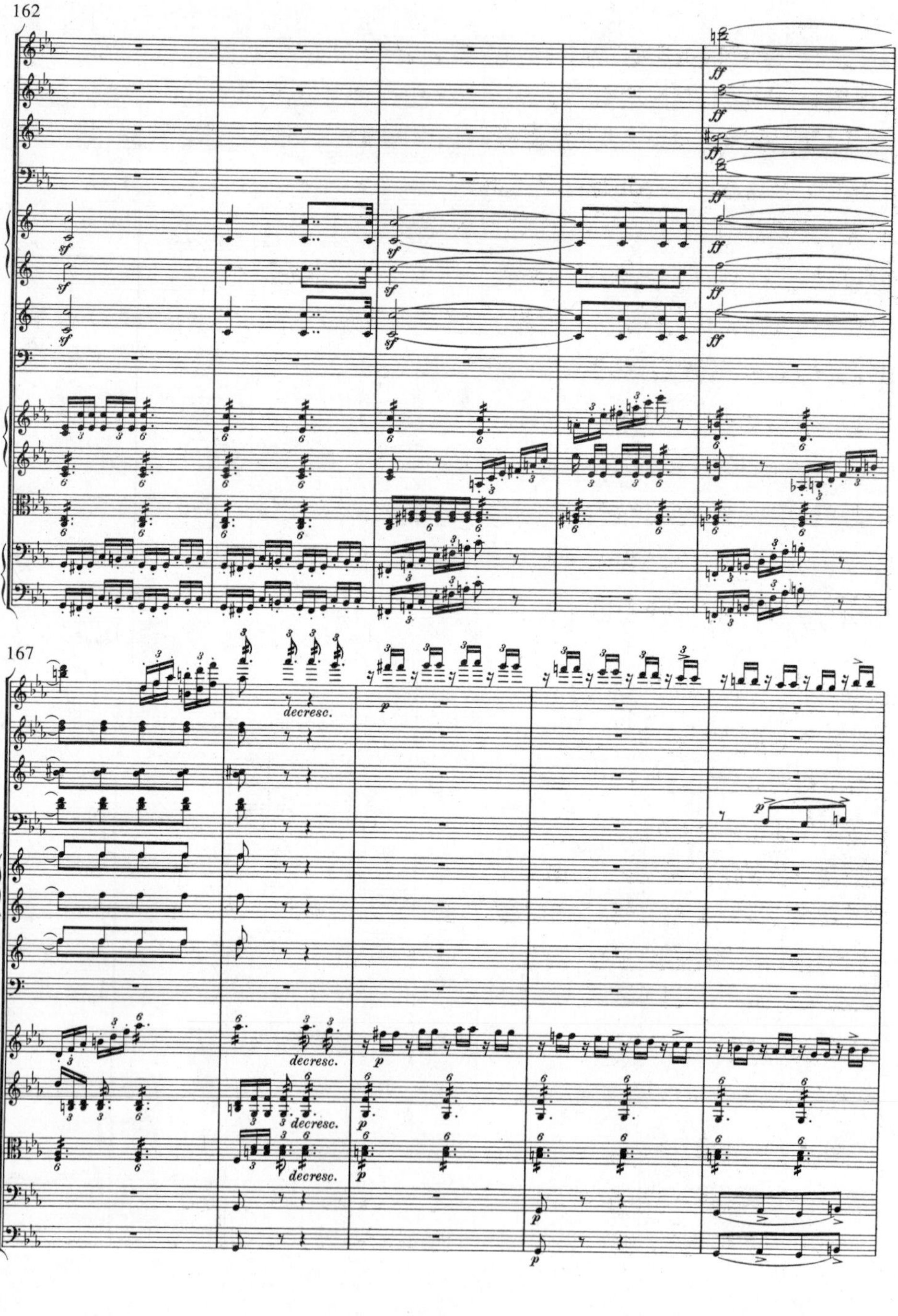
162
sf
ff
167
decresc.
p

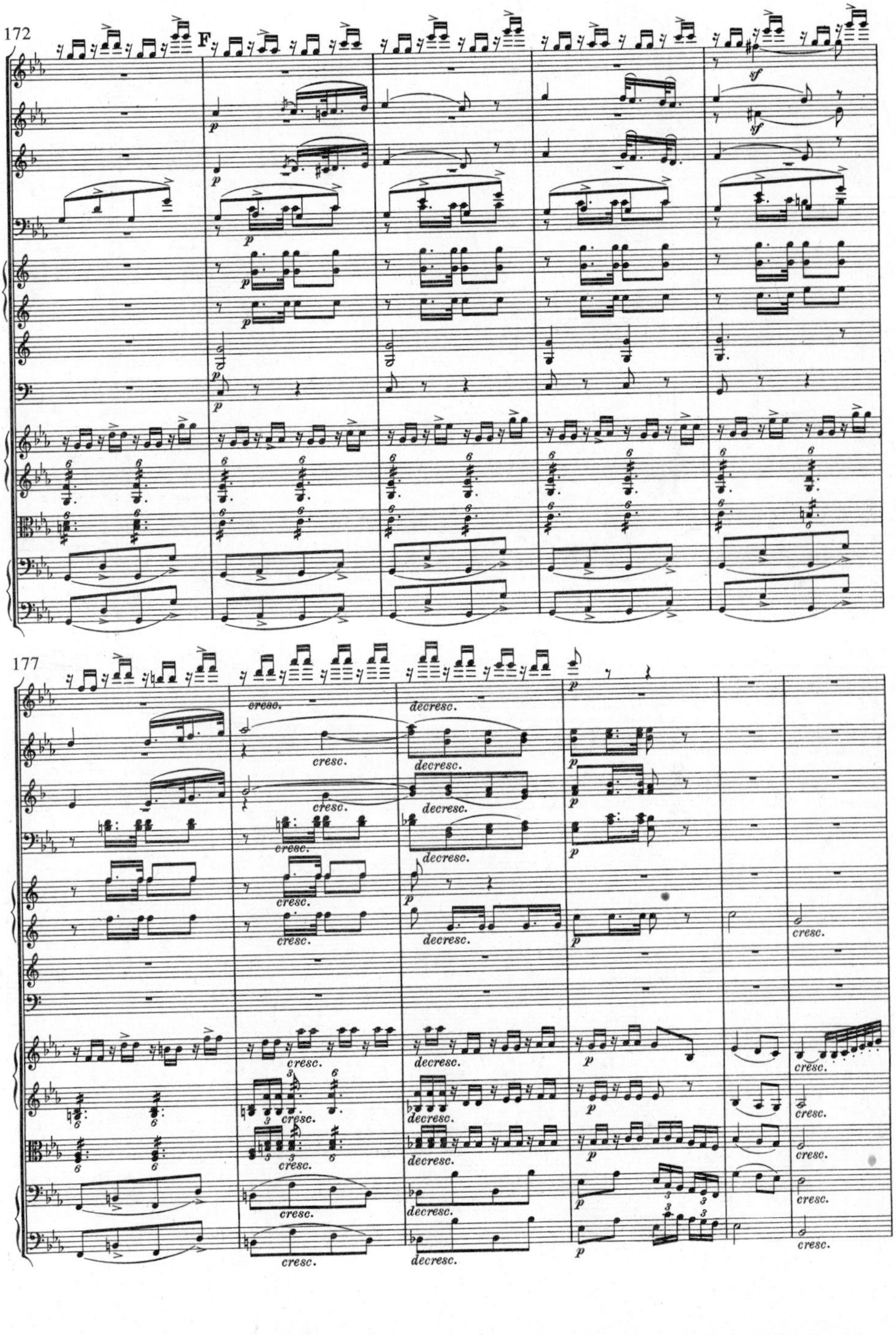
172
F
p
sf
177
cresc.
decresc.
p

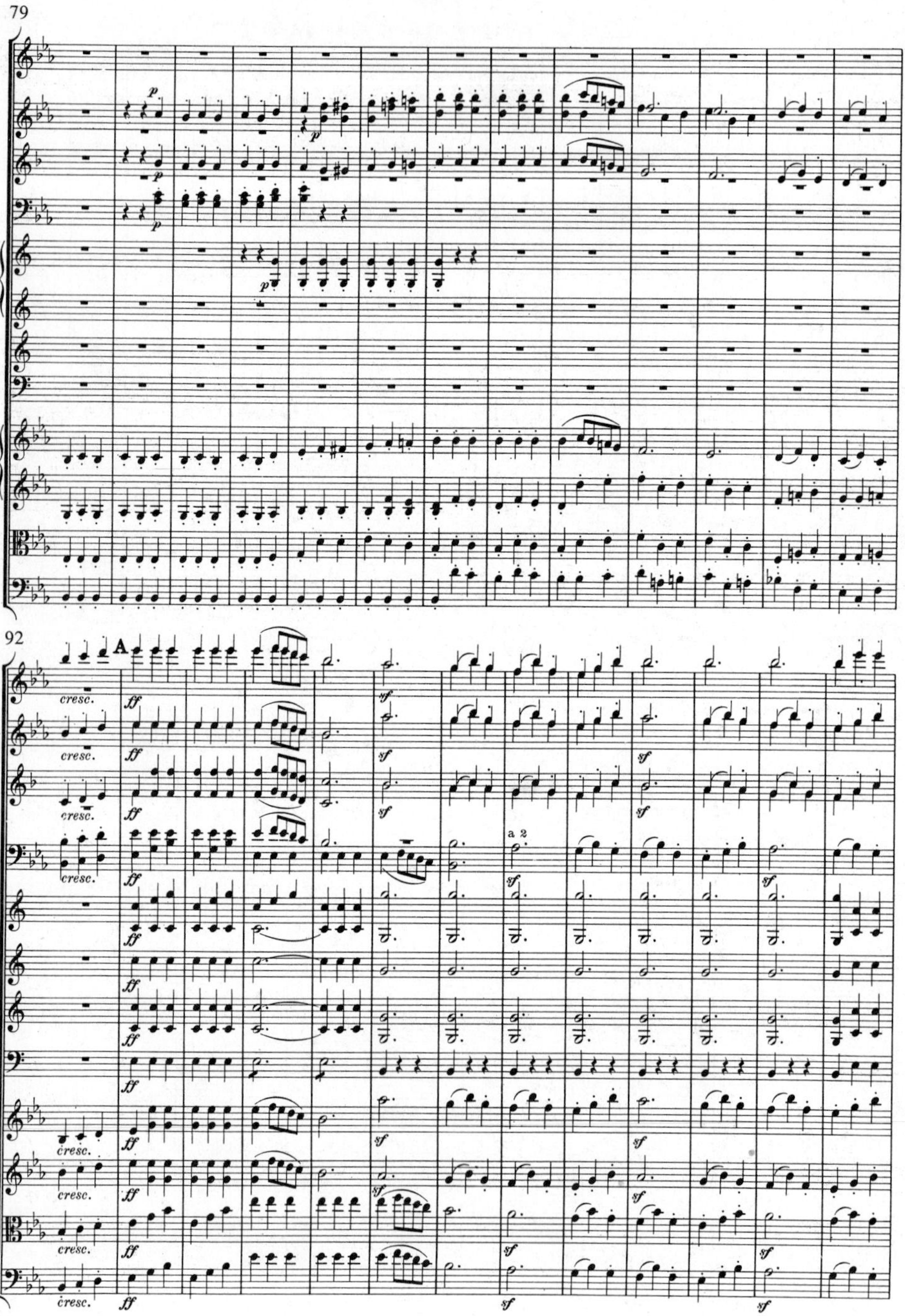
79
p
92
A
cresc.
ff
sf
a 2

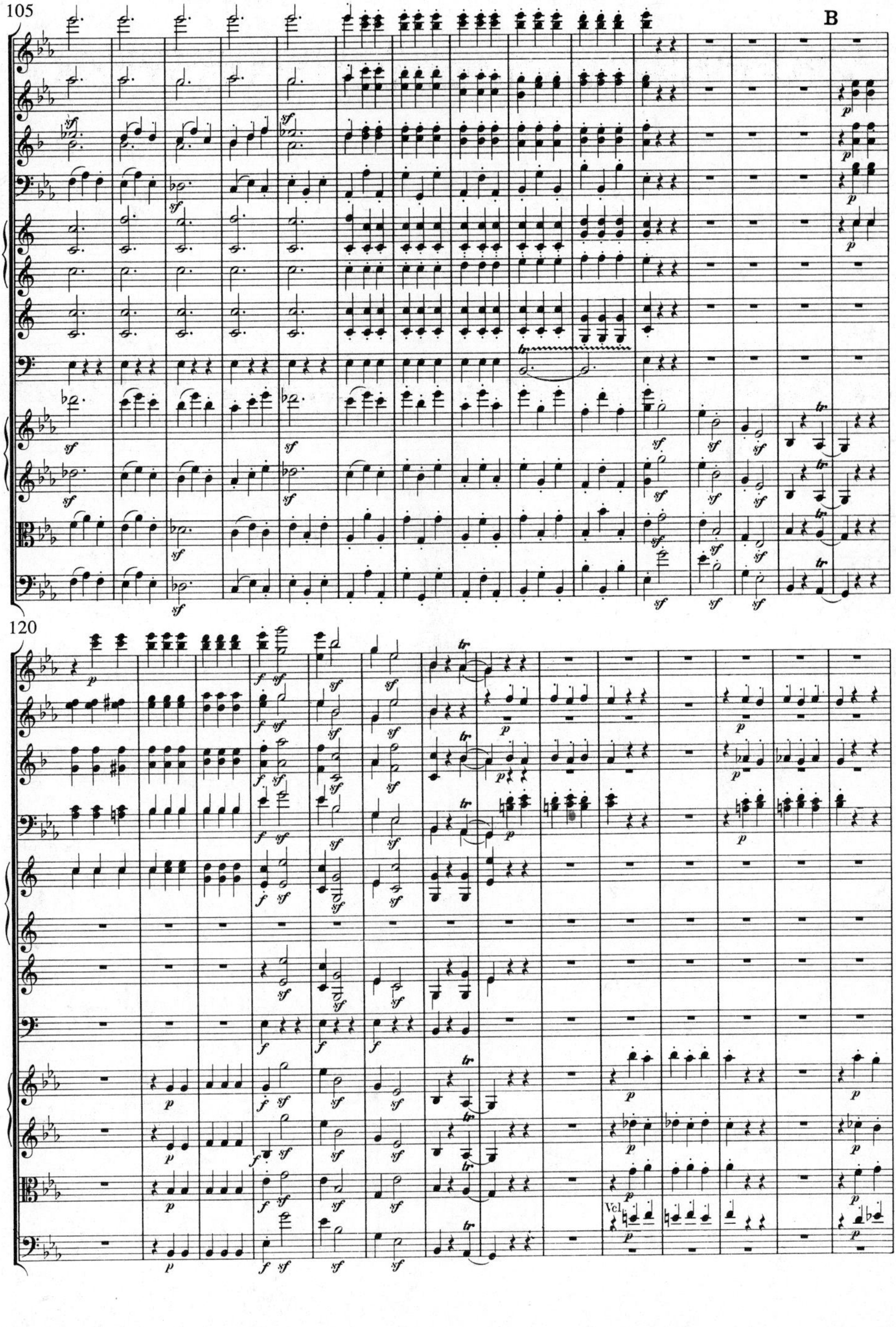
105
B
120
Vcl.

IV

Finale
Allegro molto ($\diamond$ = 76)

54

66

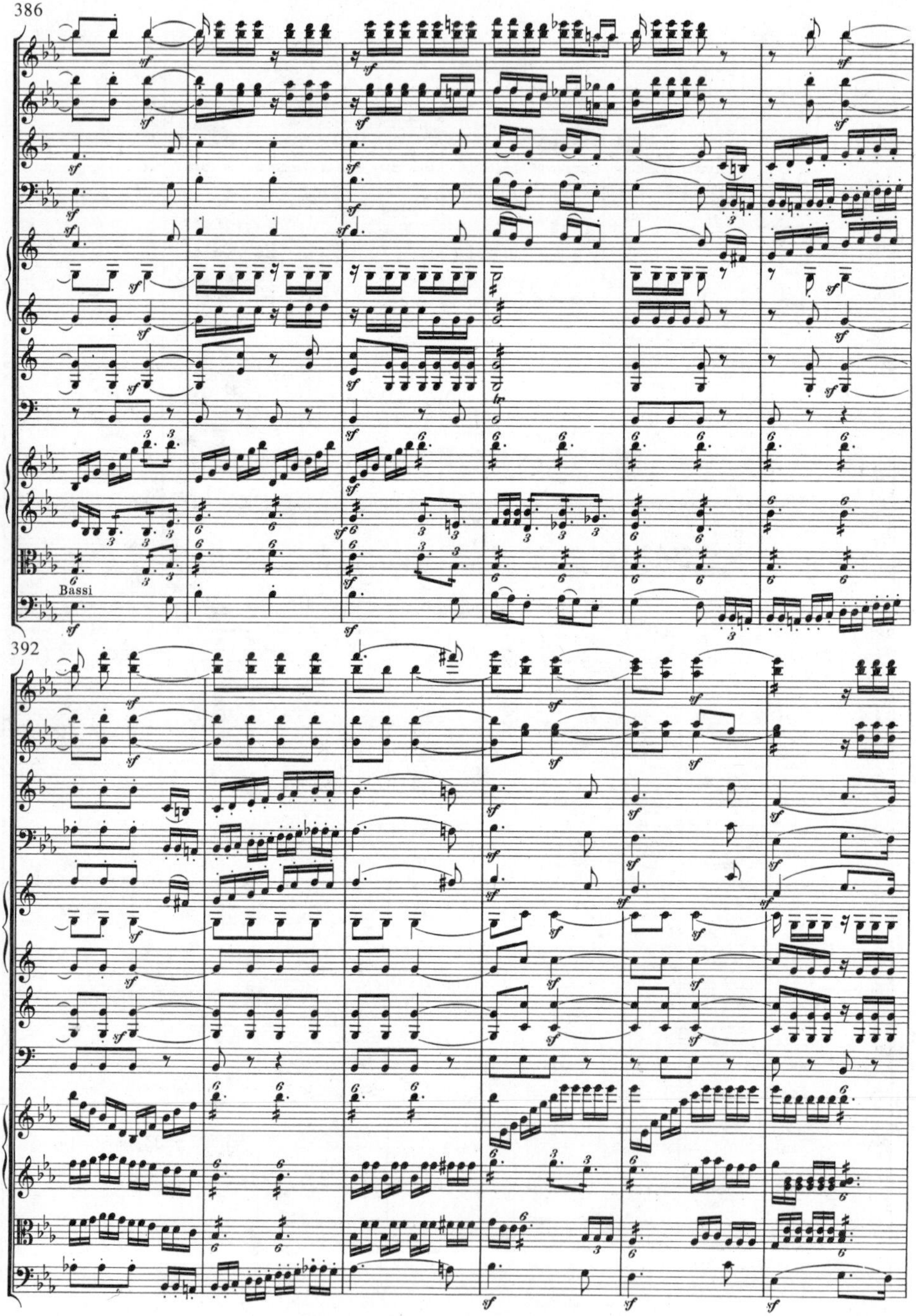
386
Bassi
392

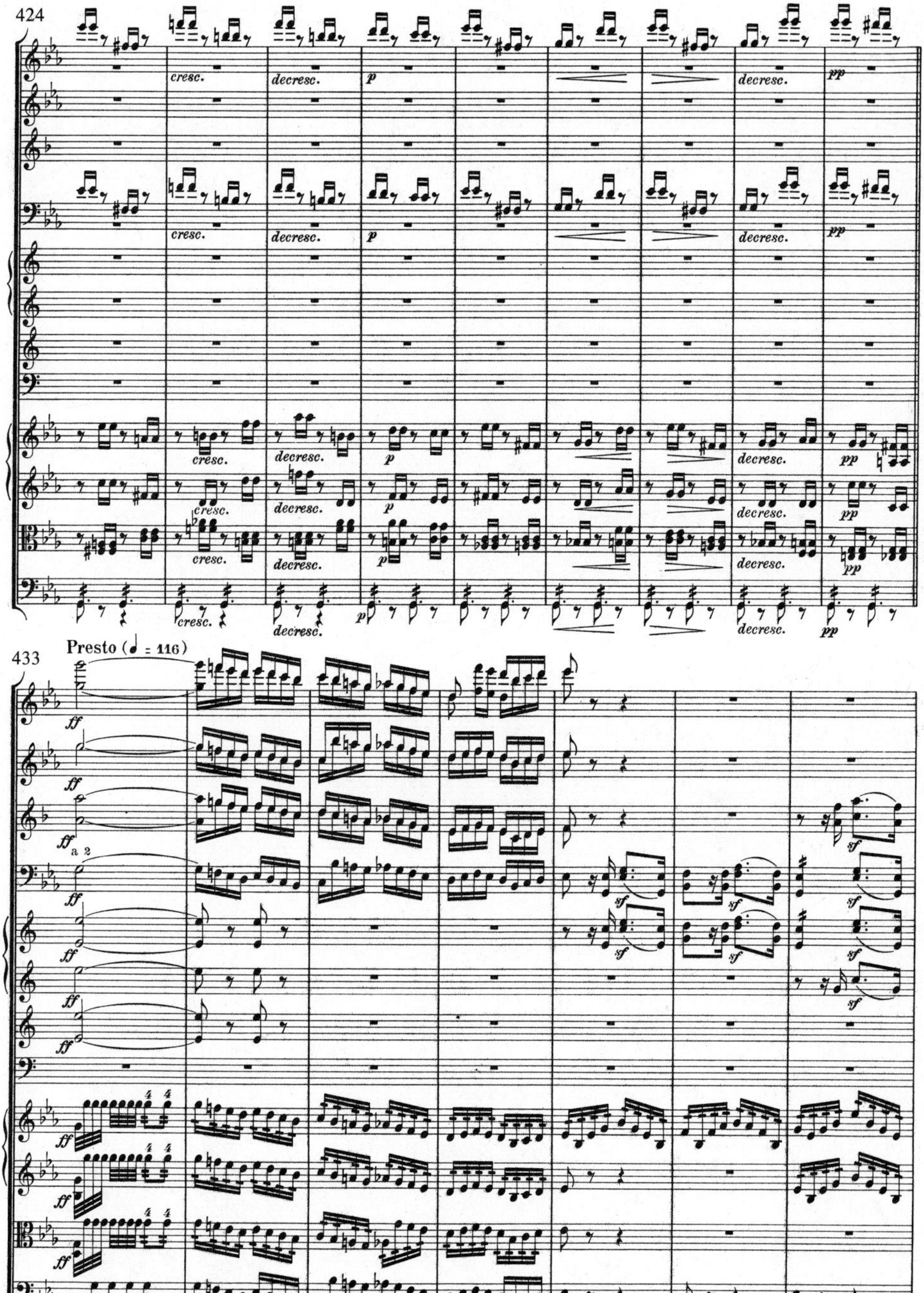
424
cresc.
decresc.
p
decresc.
pp
433
Presto (♩ = 116)
ff
a 2
sf

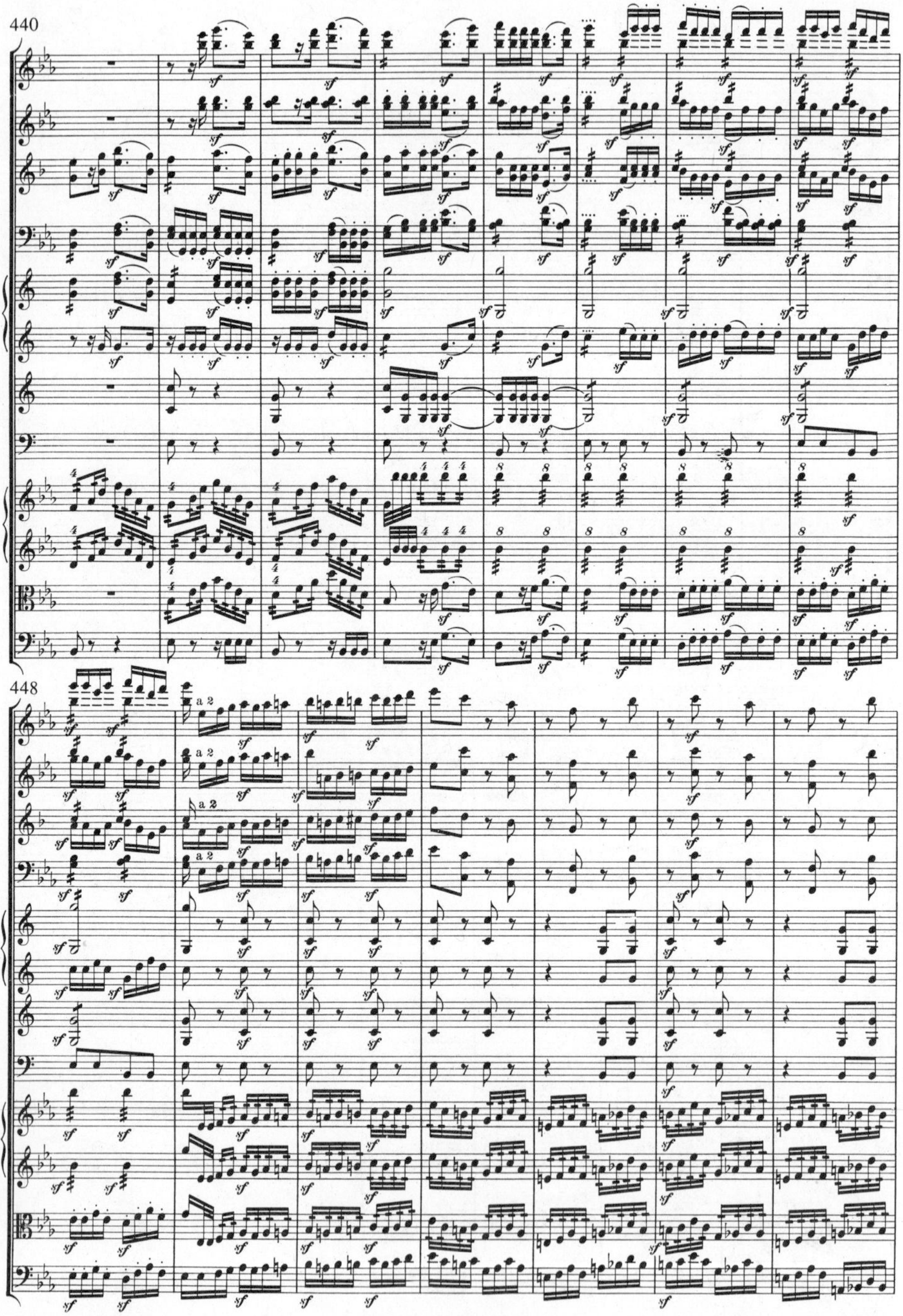
440
448
a 2
sf

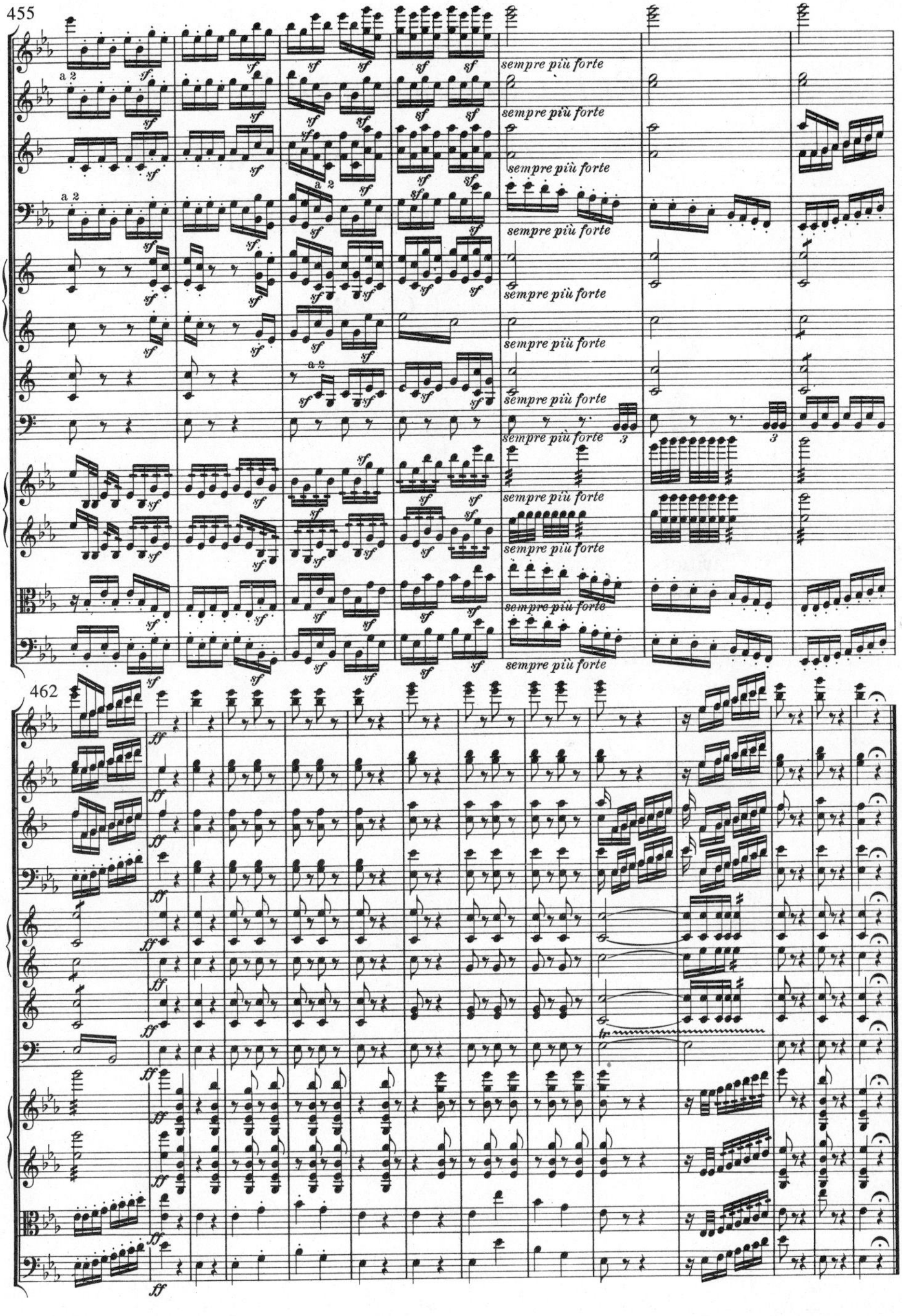
455
a 2
sempre più forte
sf
a 2
462
ff
tr

Franz Schubert (1797–1828)

SYMPHONY IN B MINOR, D. 759

("UNFINISHED")

(1822)

INSTRUMENTATION

2 Flutes
2 Oboes
2 Clarinets in A
2 Bassoons

2 Horns in D, E
2 Trumpets in E
3 Trombones

Timpani

Violin I
Violin II
Viola
Cello
Double Bass

I

II

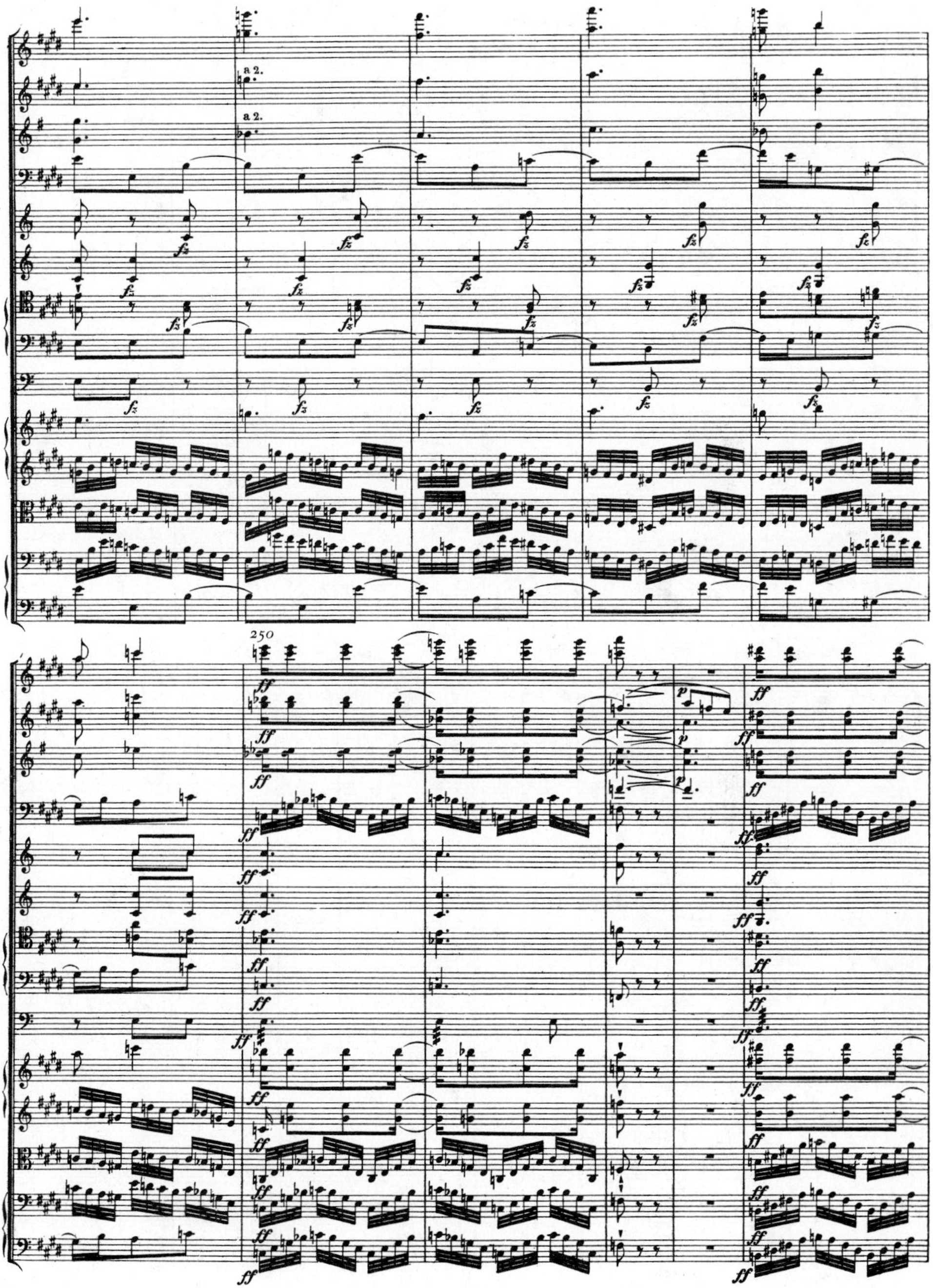
a 2.
a 2.
fz
250
ff
p

Hector Berlioz *(1803–1869)*

SYMPHONIE FANTASTIQUE

(1830, revised 1831)

INSTRUMENTATION

2 Flutes *(Fl.)*
II doubles on Piccolo *(Fl. picc.)*
2 Oboes *(Ob.)*
II doubles on English horn
    (C. ingl.)
2 Clarinets *(Clar.)* in B♭ *(B)*, A,
    C, E♭ *(Es)*
4 Bassoons *(Fag.)*

4 Horns *(Cor.)* in E♭ *(Es)*, E, F,
    B♭ *(B)*, C
2 Cornets *(Ctti.)* in B♭ *(B)*, A
2 Trumpets *(Tr.)* in C, B♭ *(B)*, E♭
    (Es)
3 Trombones *(Tromb.)*
2 Tubas

Timpani *(Timp.)*
Bass drum *(Gr. Tamb.)*
Snare drum *(Tamburo)*
Cymbals *(Cinelli)*
Bells *(Campane)*
2 Harps *(Arpa)*

Violin I *(Viol. I)*
Violin II *(Viol. II)*
Viola
Cello *(Vcello., Vcllo.)*
Double Bass *(C. B.)*

AN EPISODE IN THE LIFE OF AN ARTIST

Explanatory

The following program must be distributed among the audience whenever the *Symphonie fantastique* is played dramatically and it is followed by the lyric monodrama *Lélio*,[1] which ends and completes the episode in the life of an artist. When such a performance is given, the orchestra must be invisible and placed on the stage of a theatre behind the lowered curtain.

When the symphony is given by itself in a concert, these directions are superfluous and, strictly speaking, the distribution of this program may be dispensed with. In such cases it is only necessary to retain the titles of the five movements. The composer indulges himself with the hope that the symphony will, on its own merits and irrespective of any dramatic aim, offer an interest in the musical sense alone.

Program of the Symphony

A young musician of an unhealthily sensitive nature and endowed with vivid imagination has poisoned himself with opium in a paroxysm of love-sick despair. The narcotic dose he has taken, too weak to cause death, throws him into a long sleep accompanied by the most extraordinary visions. In this condition his sensations, feelings, and memories are translated, within his sick brain, into the form of musical thoughts and images. Even the beloved one has taken the form of melody in his mind, like a fixed idea which is ever returning and which he hears everywhere.

1st Movement / Dreams—Passions

At first he thinks of the uneasy and nervous condition of his soul, of somber longings, of depression and joyous elation without any recognisable cause, which he experienced before the beloved one had appeared to him. Then he remembers the ardent love with which she suddenly inspired him, his almost insane anxiety of mind, his raging jealousy, his reawakening love, his religious consolation.

[1] The lyric monodrama *Lélio* forms a sequel to the *Symphonie fantastique,* but is rarely performed with it. [*Editor*]

2nd Movement / *A Ball*

At a ball, amidst the confusion of a brilliant festival, he finds the loved one again.

3rd Movement / *In the Country*

On a summer evening in the country, he hears two shepherd-lads who play the *ranz des vaches* [the tune used by the Swiss to call their flocks together] in alternation. This pastoral duet, the setting, the soft whisperings of the trees stirred by the wind, some prospects of hope recently made known to him—all these sensations unite to impart an unaccustomed repose to his heart and to lend a smiling color to his imagination. And then she appears once more. His heart stops beating, painful forebodings fill his soul. "If she should prove false to him!" One of the shepherds resumes the melody, but the other no longer answers. . . . Sunset . . . distant rolling of thunder . . . loneliness . . . silence.

4th Movement / *March to the Scaffold*

He dreams that he has murdered his beloved, that he has been condemned to death and is being led to the scaffold. The procession advances, accompanied by a march that is alternately sombre and wild, brilliant and solemn, in which the sound of heavy steps follows without transition upon the most tumultuous outbursts. At last the fixed idea returns for a moment as the last thought of love is cut short by the fatal stroke.

5th Movement
 Dream of a Witches' Sabbath

He dreams that he is present at a witches' dance, surrounded by horrible spirits, amidst sorcerers and monsters in many fearful forms, who have come to assist at his funeral. Strange sounds, groans, shrill laughter, distant yells, which other cries seem to answer. The beloved melody is heard again but it has lost its noble and shy character; it has become a vulgar, trivial and grotesque dance-tune. *She* it is, who comes to attend the witches' meeting. Howls of joy greet her arrival. . . . She joins the infernal orgy. . . . Bells toll for the dead, a burlesque parody of the *Dies irae.* The witches' round-dance. The dance and the *Dies irae* are heard at the same time.

I

Dreams and Passions

Une mesure de ce **mouvement** équivaut au quart de la précédente.
Ein Takt dieses Zeitmaßes wie ein Viertel des vorhergehenden.
One bar of this time-measure is equal to a quarter-bar of the preceding movement.

64 **Allegro agitato e appassionato assai** (♩ = 132)

Allegro agitato e appassionato assai. (♩ = 132.)

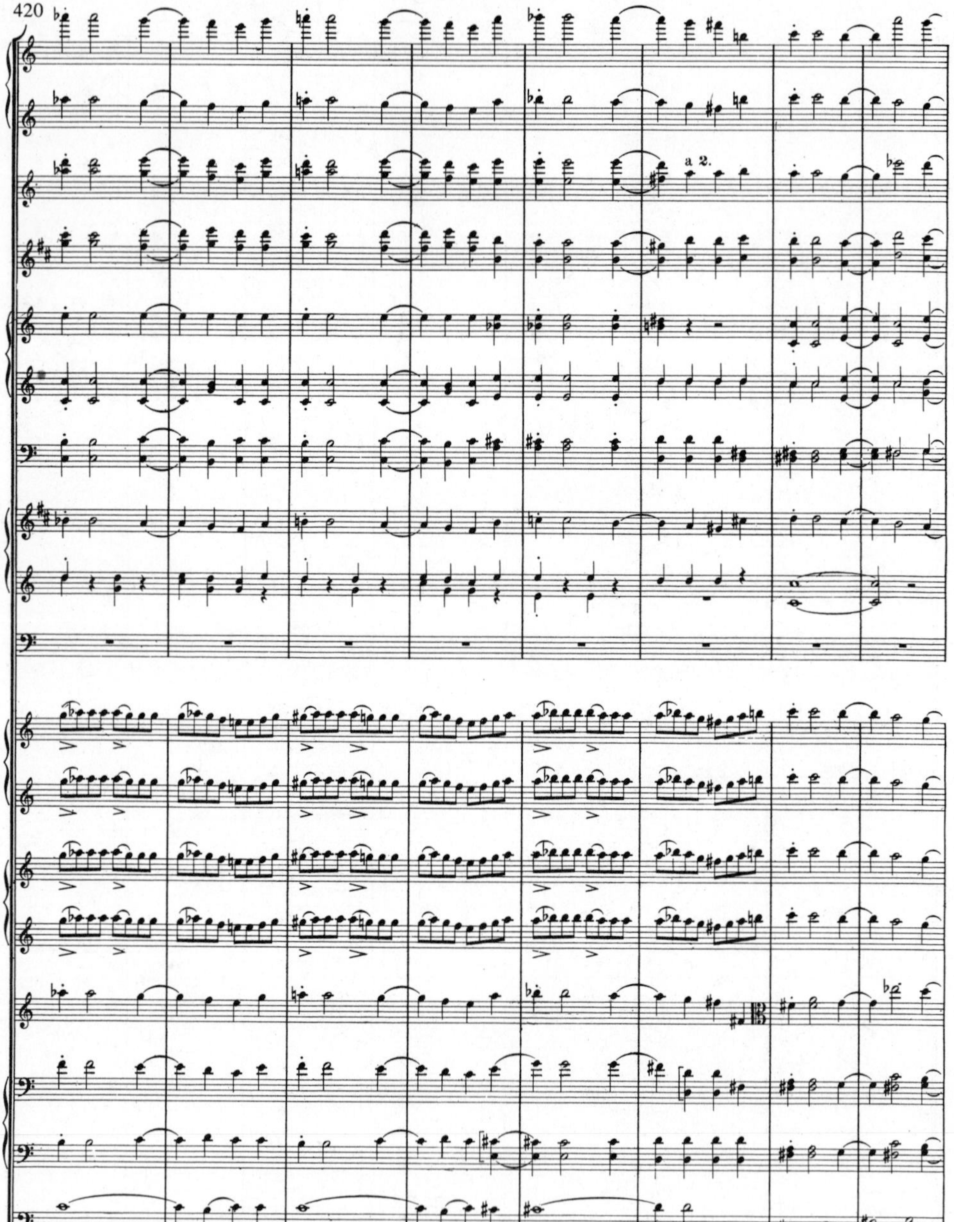
420
a 2.

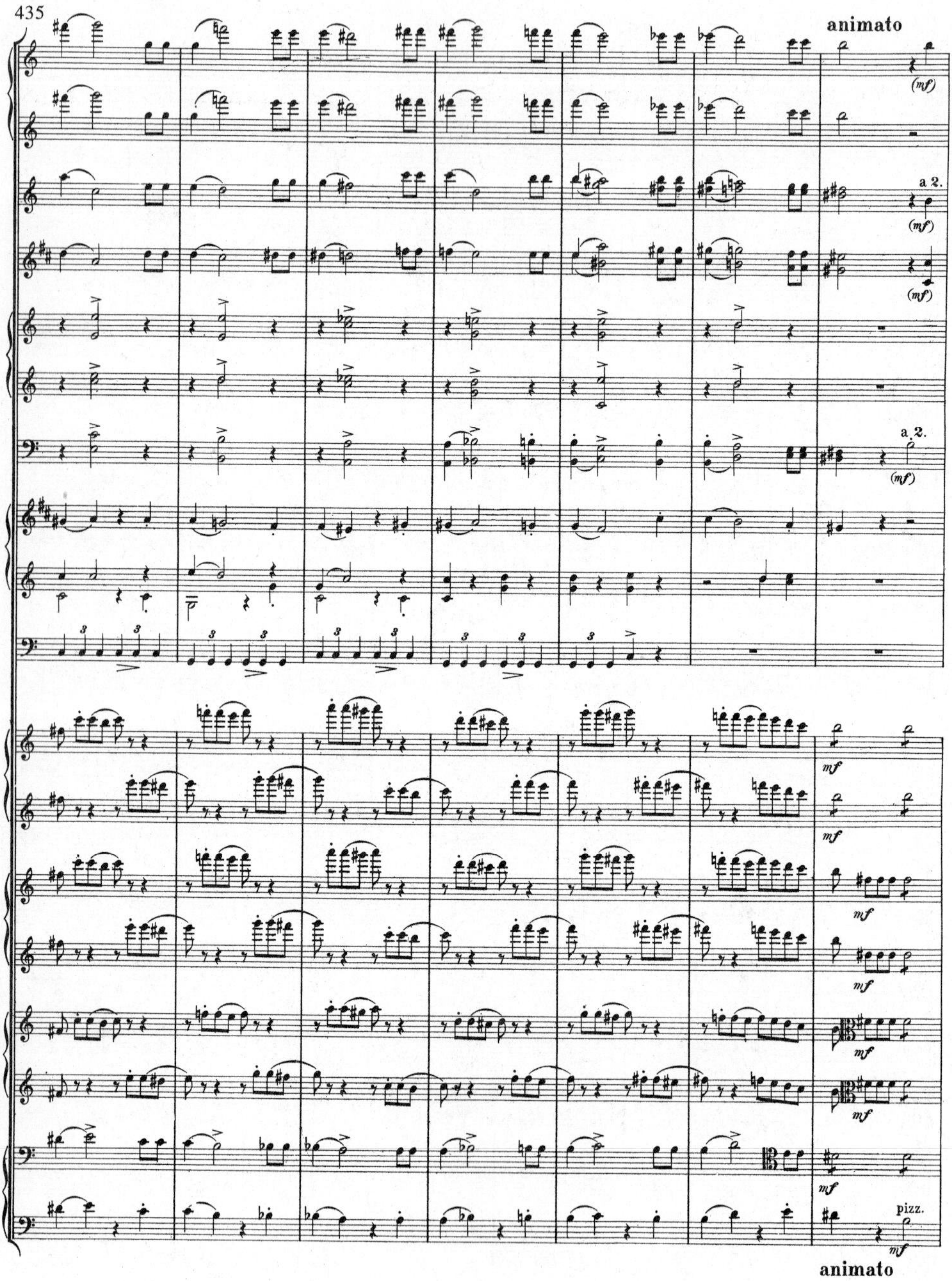
435
animato
(mf)
a 2.
(mf)
(mf)
a 2.
(mf)
mf
mf
mf
mf
mf
mf
mf
pizz.
mf
animato

II

A Ball

138
Fl.
cresc. poco a poco
Clar.
cresc. poco a poco
(ppp)
Viol.
(sempre ppp)
(ppp)
(sempre ppp)
(sempre ppp)
147
Fl.
Clar.
cresc.
poco f
cresc.
poco f
cresc.
157
27
Fl.
I.
p
pp
dimin.
Ob.
ppp
Clar.
I.
p
ppp.
pp
dimin.
Cor.
pp
cresc. poco a poco
cresc. poco a poco
p
(p)
Viol.
p
pp
dimin.
p
pp
dimin.
p
pp
dimin.
Vello.
(p
pp)
dimin.
C. B.
27

185
Fl.
Ob.
Clar.
Cor. I. II.
Ctto
Arpa II.
Viol.
191
Fl.
p cresc.
f
Ob.
Clar.
Cor. I. II.
Ctto
poco f
Arpa I.
mf
(p)
Arpa II.
Viol.
poco f
Vcllo. I.
pizz.
cresc.
Vcllo. II.
C. B.

216
Fl.
Ob.
Clar.
Cor. I.II.
Arpa II.
Viol.
cresc. poco
a poco
cresc. molto
cresc.
arco
poco f
pizz.
224
Fl.
Ob.
Clar.
Cor. I. II.
Ctto
Arpa I.
Viol.
Flauto piccolo
(pp)
G.P.
pizz.
arco
G.P

269

285

342

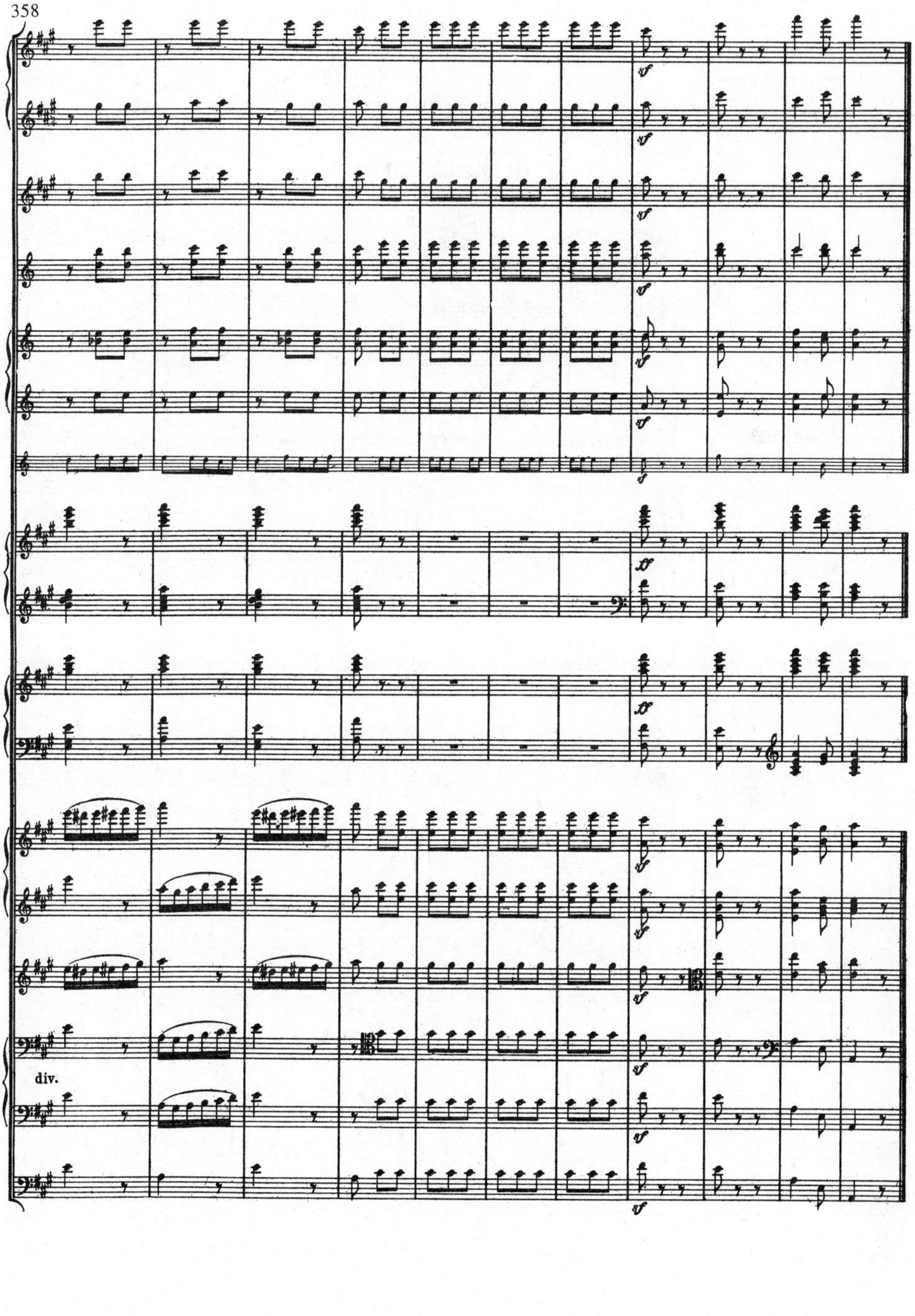
358
sf
ff
div.

III

In the Country

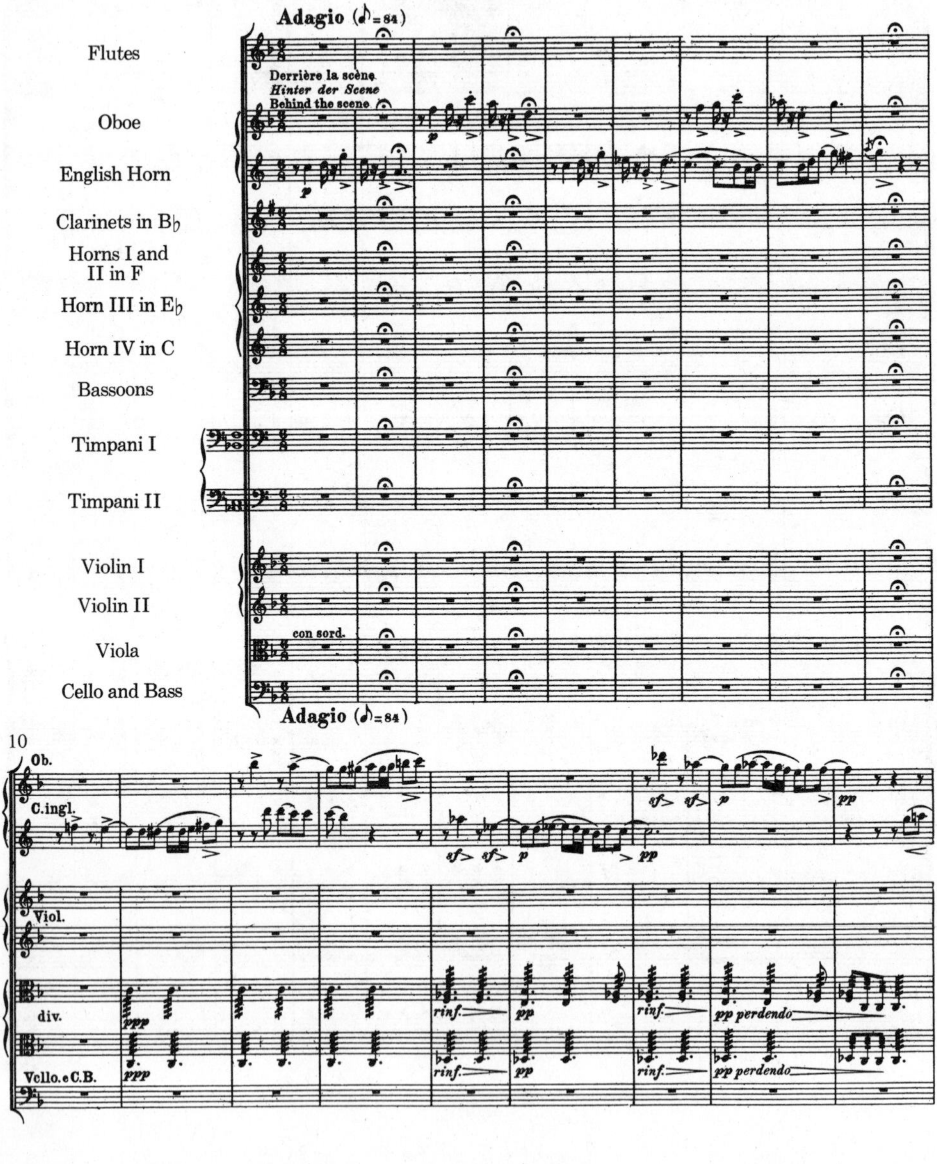

52
Fl.
cresc.
sf
p
Ob.
cresc.
p
sf
Clar.
cresc.
p
sf
Cor. I. II.
Fag.
sf
p
Viol.
cresc.
f
p
arco
pizz.
p
59
Fl.
Ob. I. II.
Clar.
Cor. IV. (in C)
Fag.
a 2.
cresc.
mf
cresc.
f
39
Viol.
unis.
cresc.
f dim.
f
arco
mf
cresc.
f
39

IV
March to the Scaffold

7

91

119

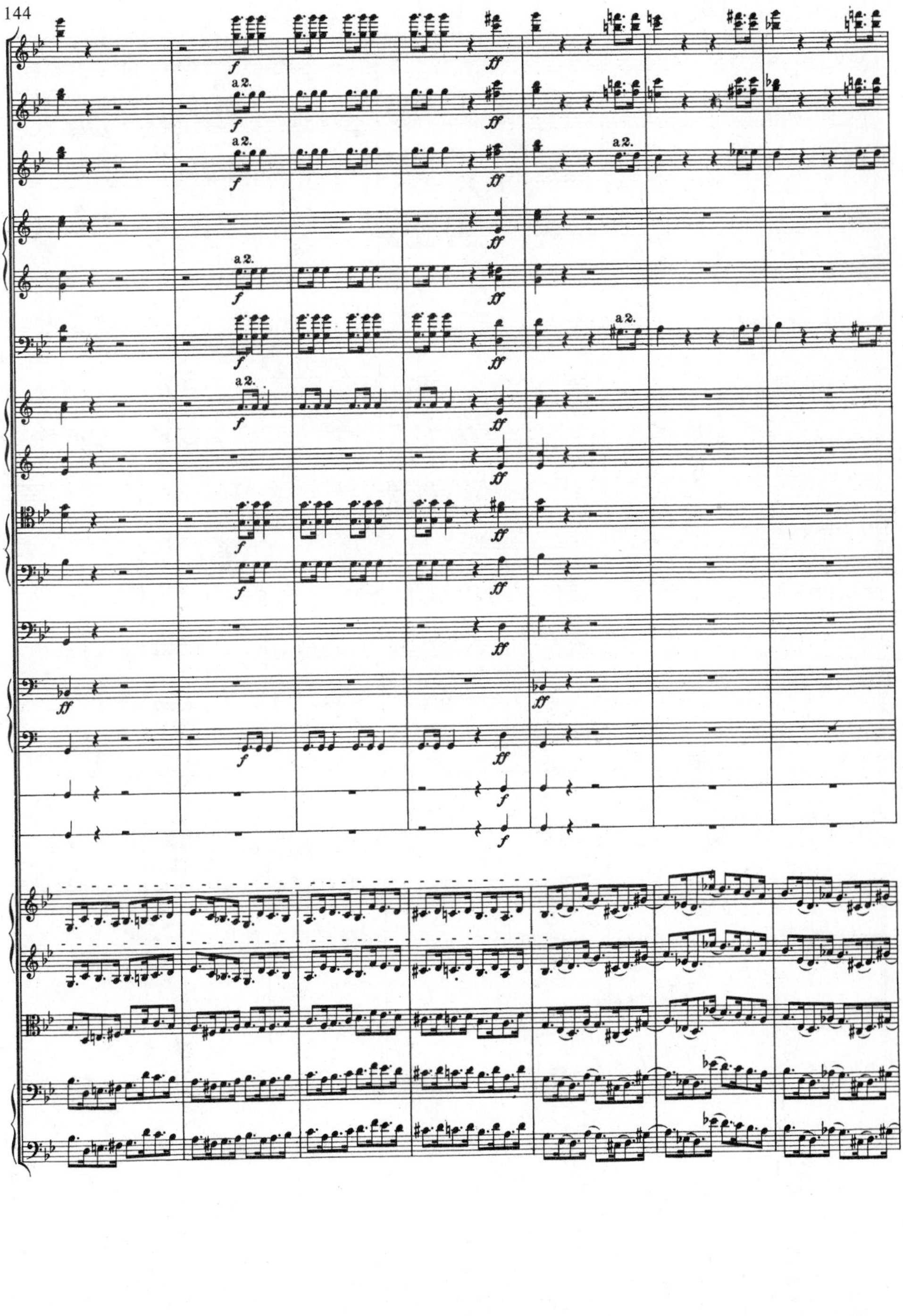
144
a2.
a2.
a2.
a2.
a2.
a2.
a2.

167

V

Dream of a Witches' Sabbath

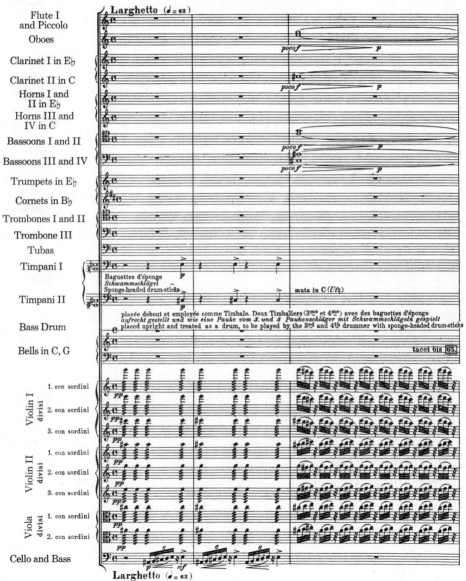

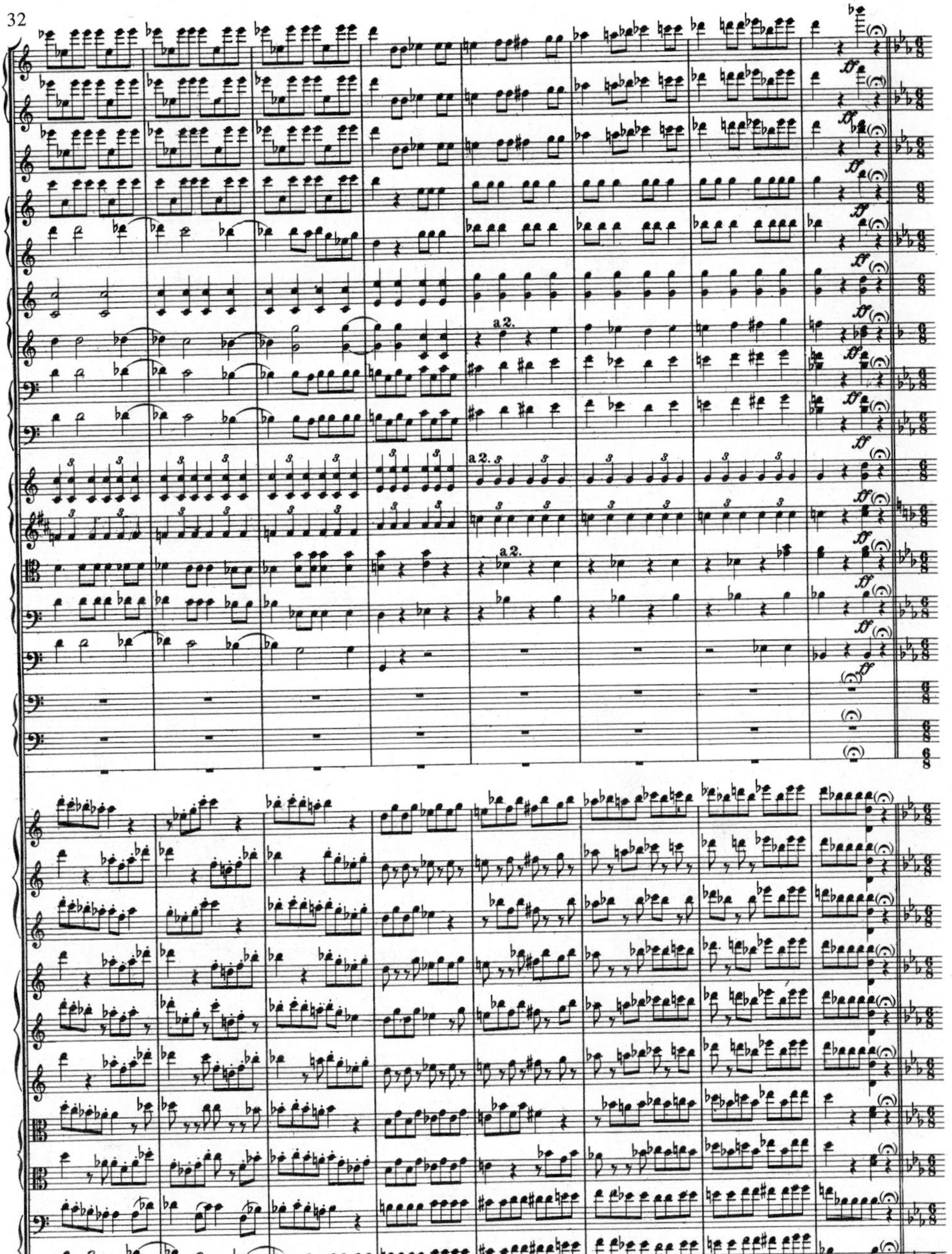
32
a 2.
a 2.
a 2.
ff

55
Fl. I.
(mf cresc.)
Fl. picc.
Ob.
a 2.
Clar.
Cor.
Fag.
Viol.
(cresc.)
(mf)
mf
61
64
Fl.
Fl. pic.
Ob.
Clar.
Cor.
Fag.
Viol.
cresc.
(cresc.)
(cresc. sempre)
ff
64

67
Fl. I.
Fl. picc.
Ob.
Clar.
Cor.
Fag.
a 4.
Tr.
Ctti
Tromb.
Tuba I.
Timp.
Viol.
a 2.
a 2.

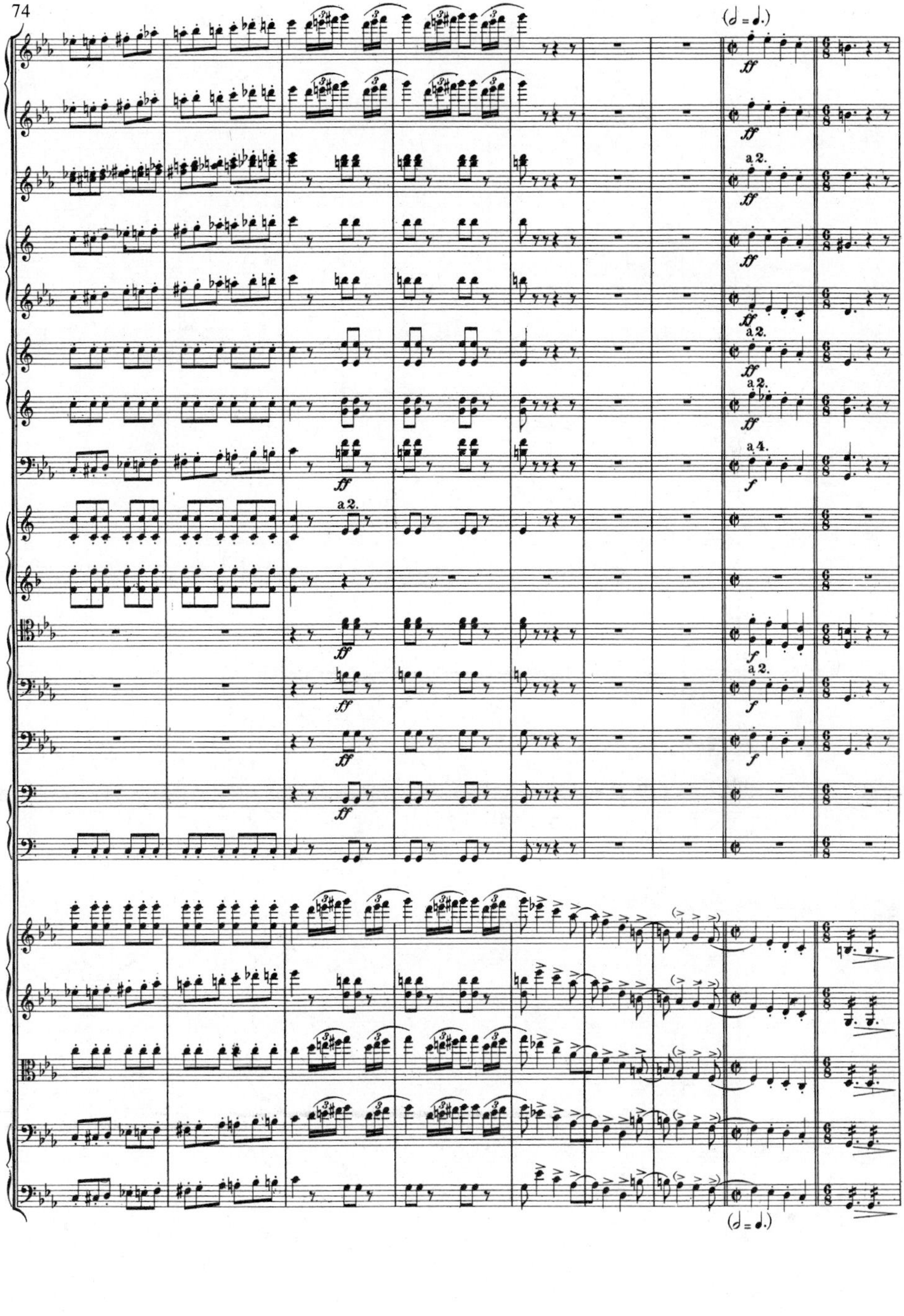
74
(𝅗𝅥 = ♩.)
ff
a 2.
a 4.
f
(𝅗𝅥 = ♩.)

146

171

184

196

Witches' round dance
241 **Poco meno mosso**

Poco meno mosso

250

272

306

327

335

345

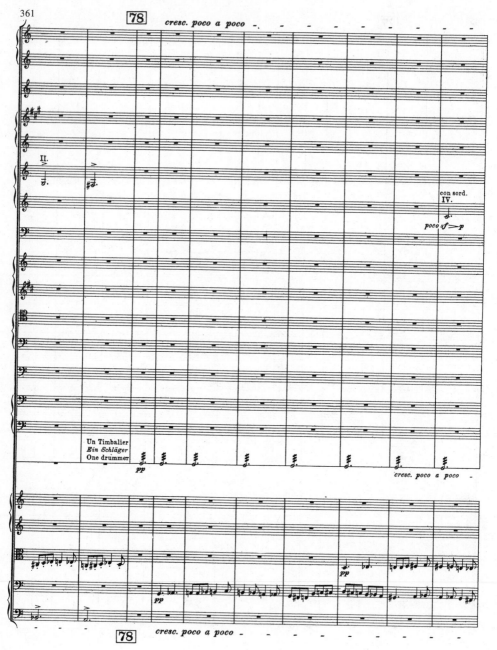

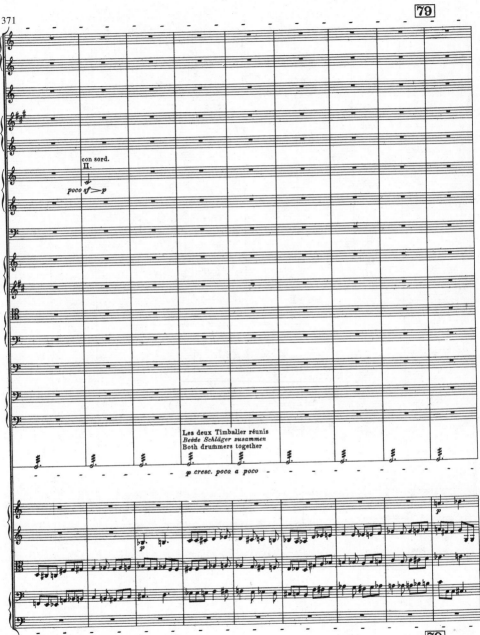

80
389
(cresc. molto)
mf (cresc. molto)
f
a 4.
ff
a 2.
cresc. molto
div.
unis.
80

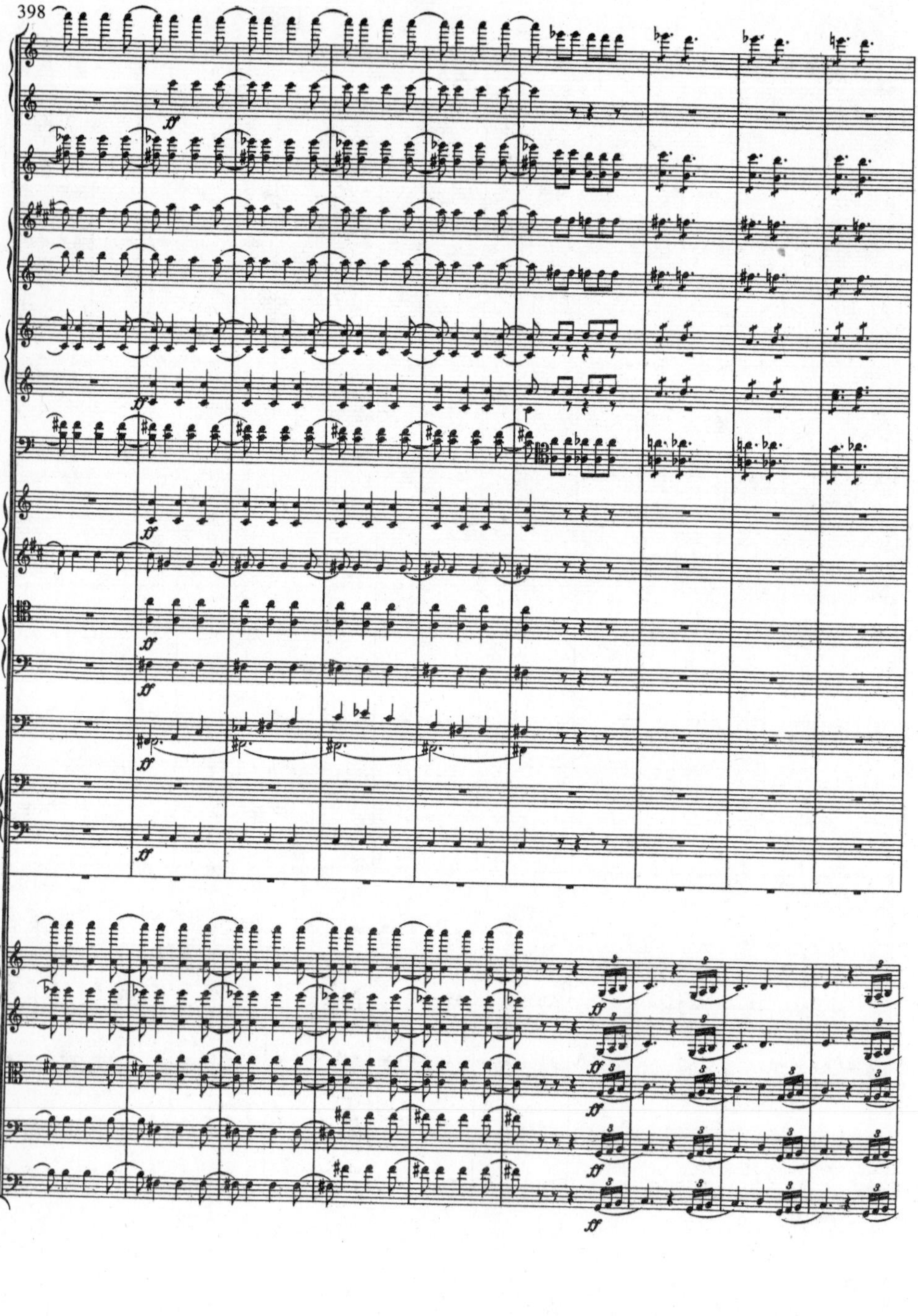
398
ff

414 **Dies irae and witches' round dance (together).**

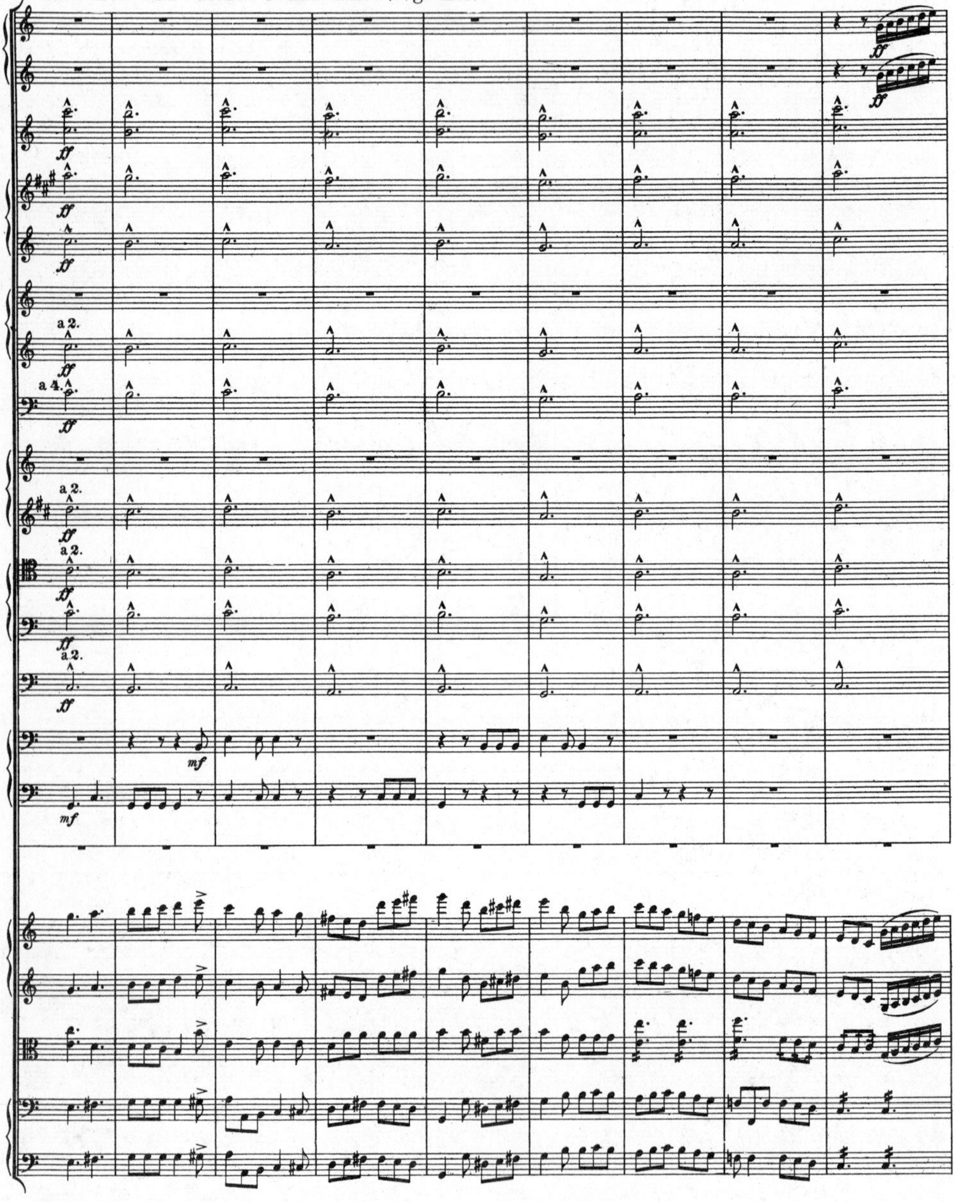

423

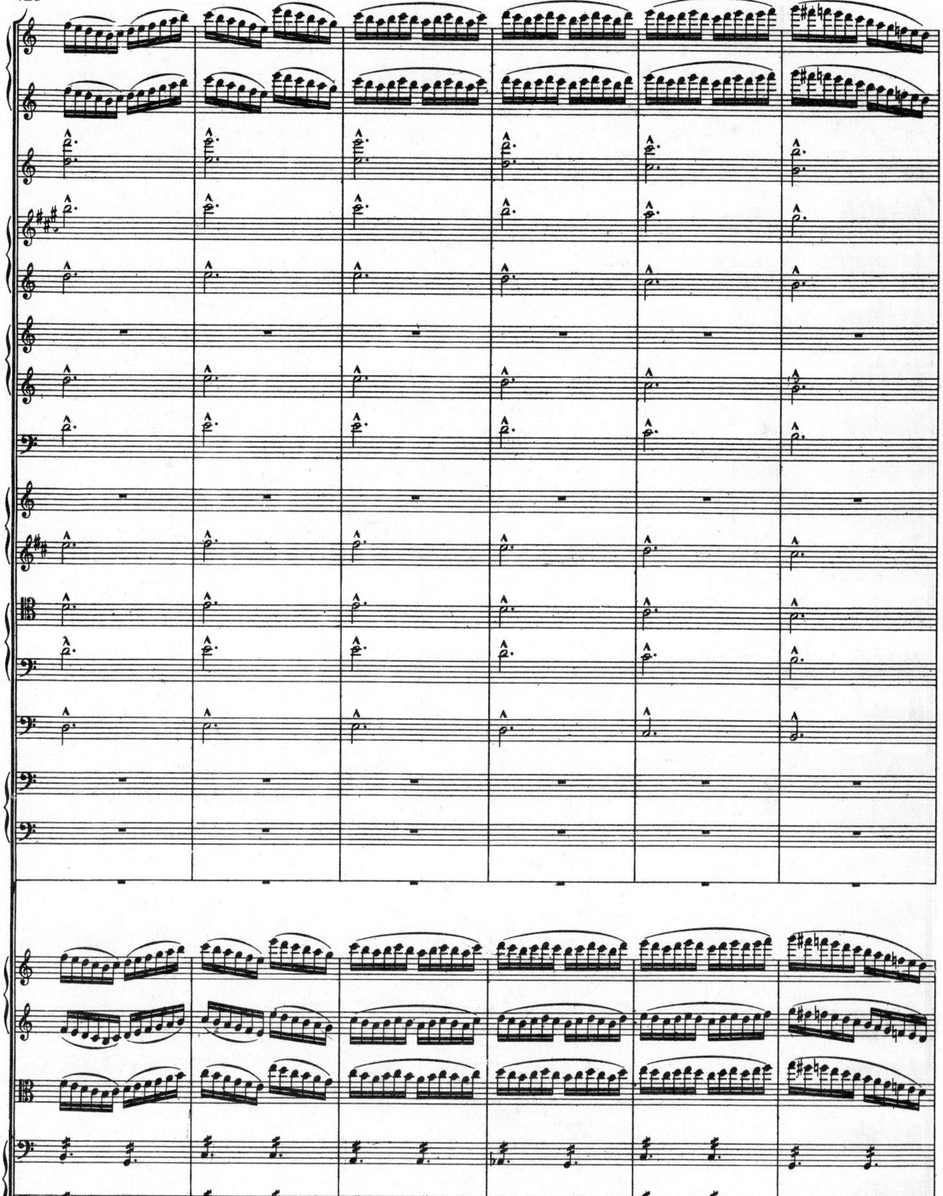

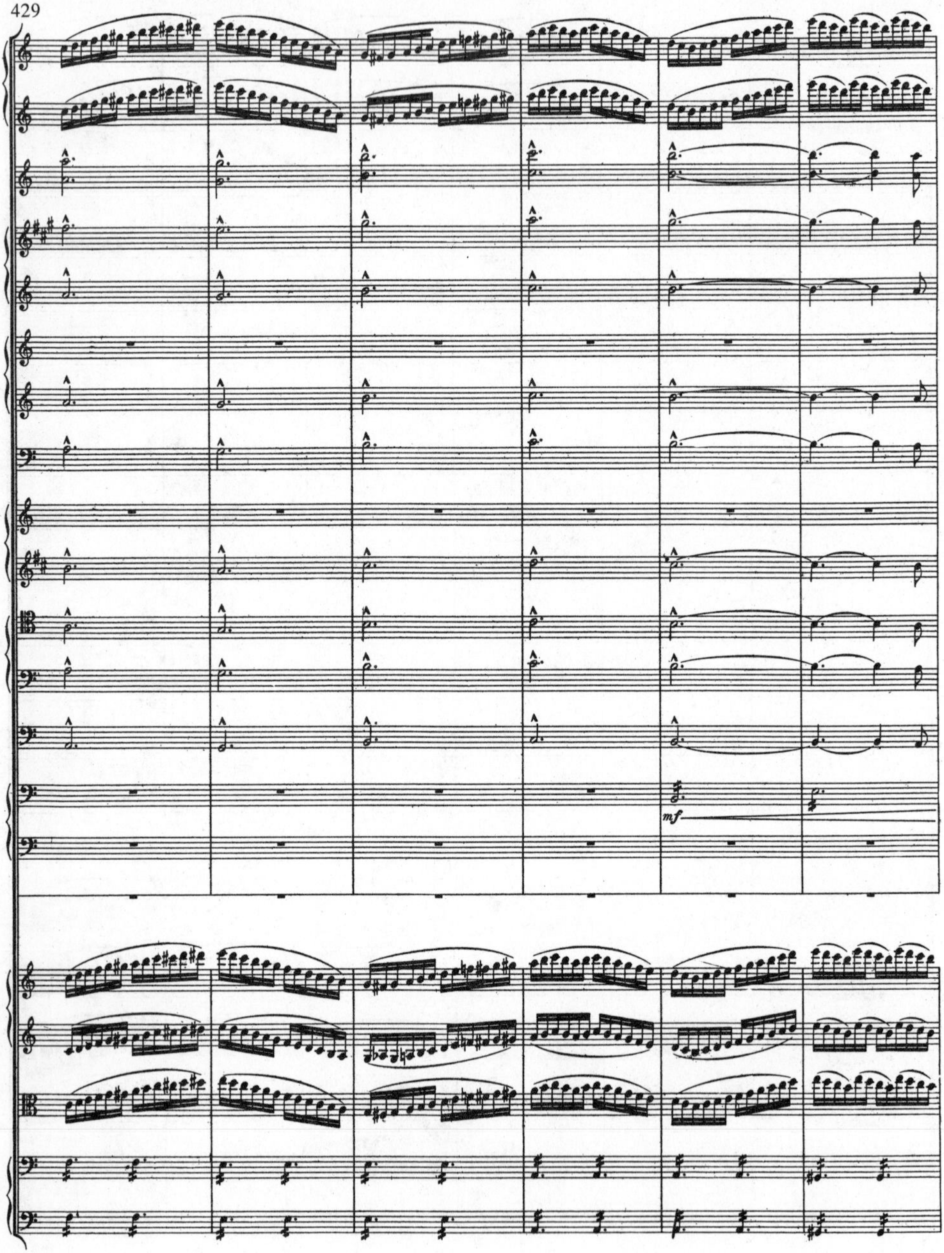
429
mf

448

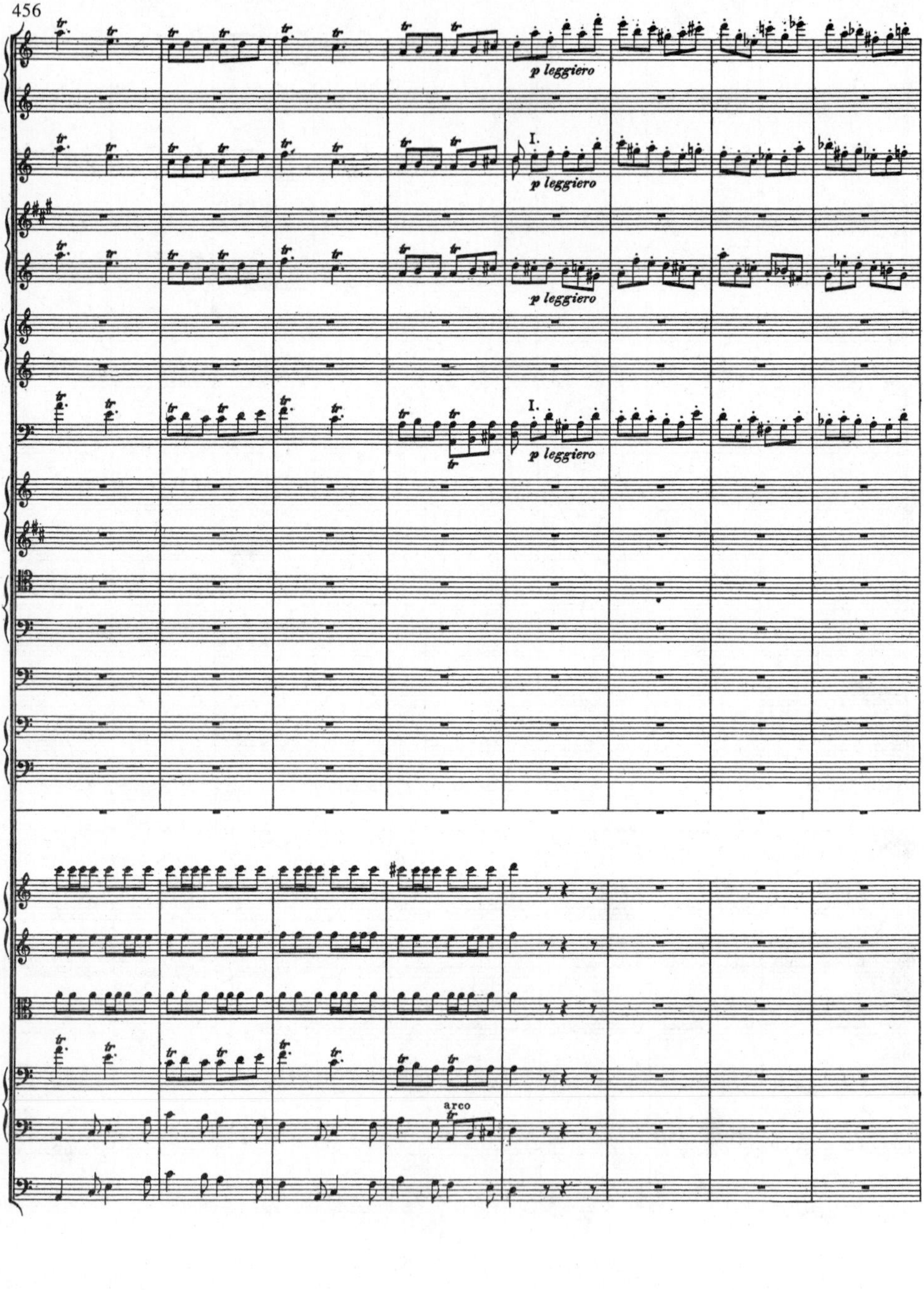
456
p leggiero
I.
p leggiero
p leggiero
I.
p leggiero
arco

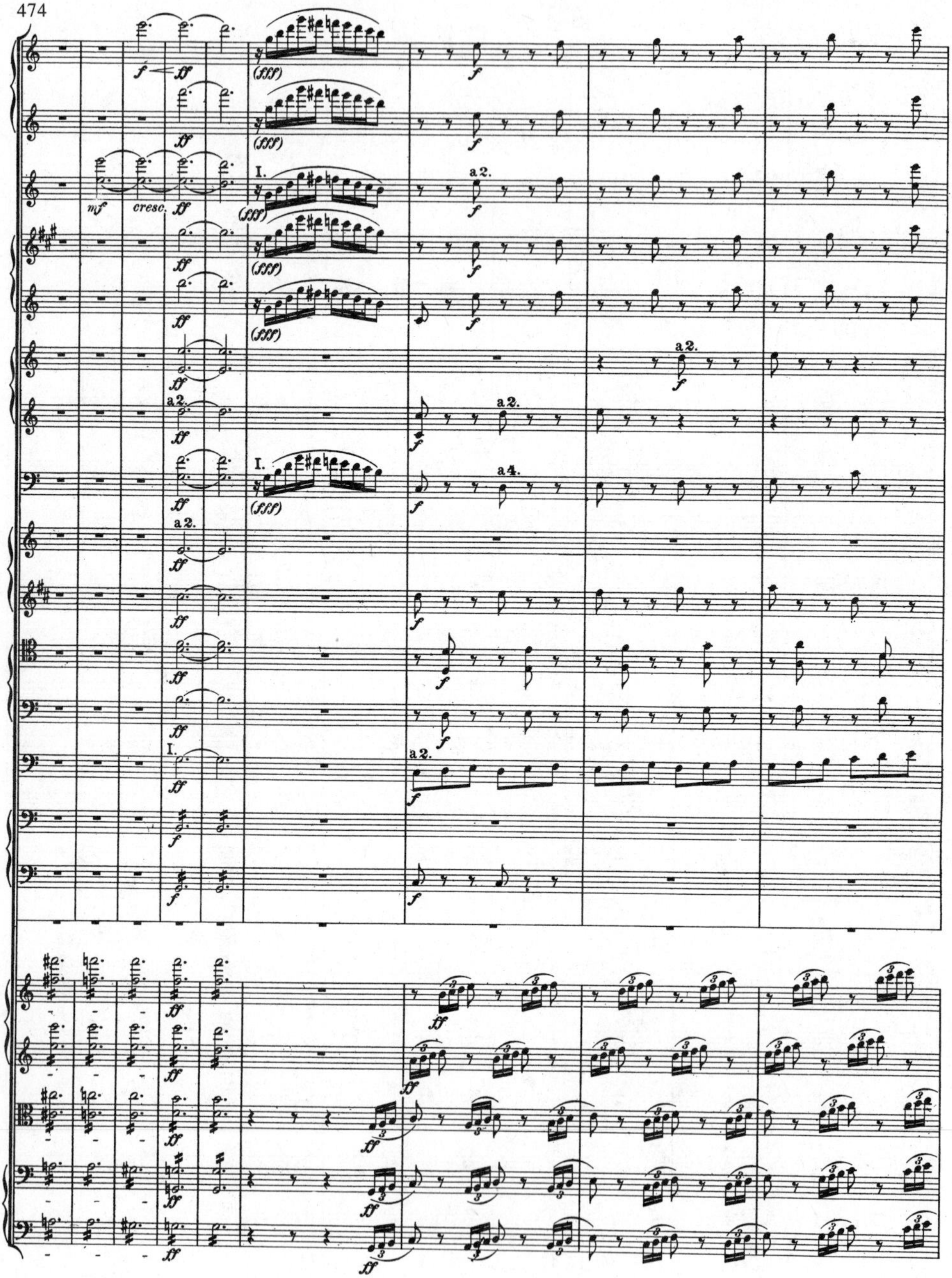
474
f
ff
(fff)
mf
cresc.
I.
a2.
a4.

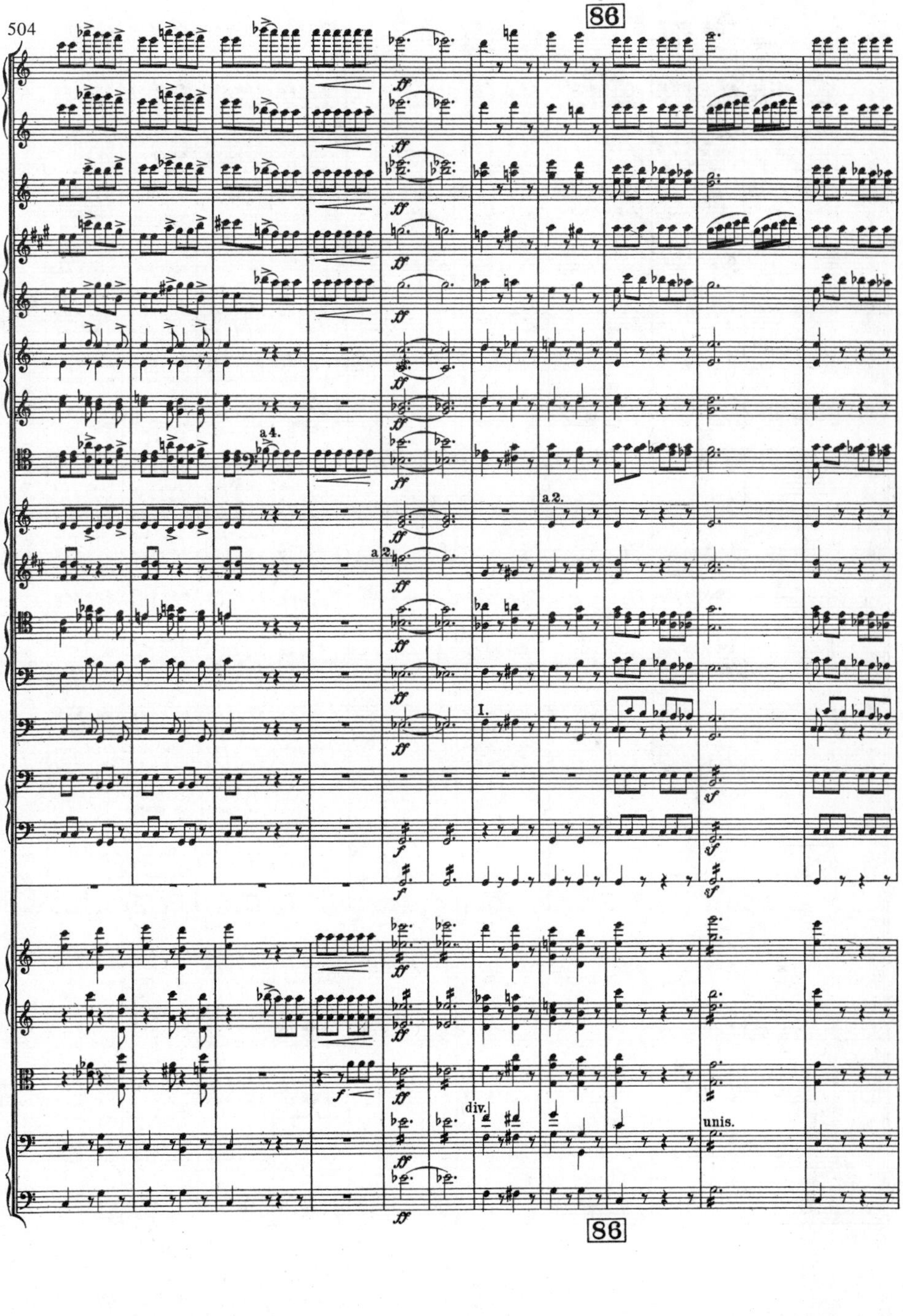
504
86
a 4.
a 2.
a 2
I.
div.
unis.
86

Coup frappé sur une Cymbale avec une baguette
couverte d'éponge ou un tampon
*Schlag auf ein Becken mit einem Schwamm-
schlägel oder Klöppel*
Struck on a cymbal with a sponge-headed
drum-stick

Cinelli.

Felix Mendelssohn *(1809–1847)*

SYMPHONY NO. 4 IN A MAJOR, OP. 90 ("ITALIAN")

(1833)

INSTRUMENTATION

2 Flutes
2 Oboes
2 Clarinets in A
2 Bassoons

2 Horns in A, E
2 Trumpets in D, E

Timpani

Violin I
Violin II
Viola
Cello
Double Bass

I

33

43

54
a 2
a 2
a 2
a 2
sf
sf
sf
sf
sf
sf
sf
sf
sf
sf
sf
sf
sf
65
sf
sf
sf
sf
mf
sf stacc.
sf
sf stacc.
sf
ff
ff

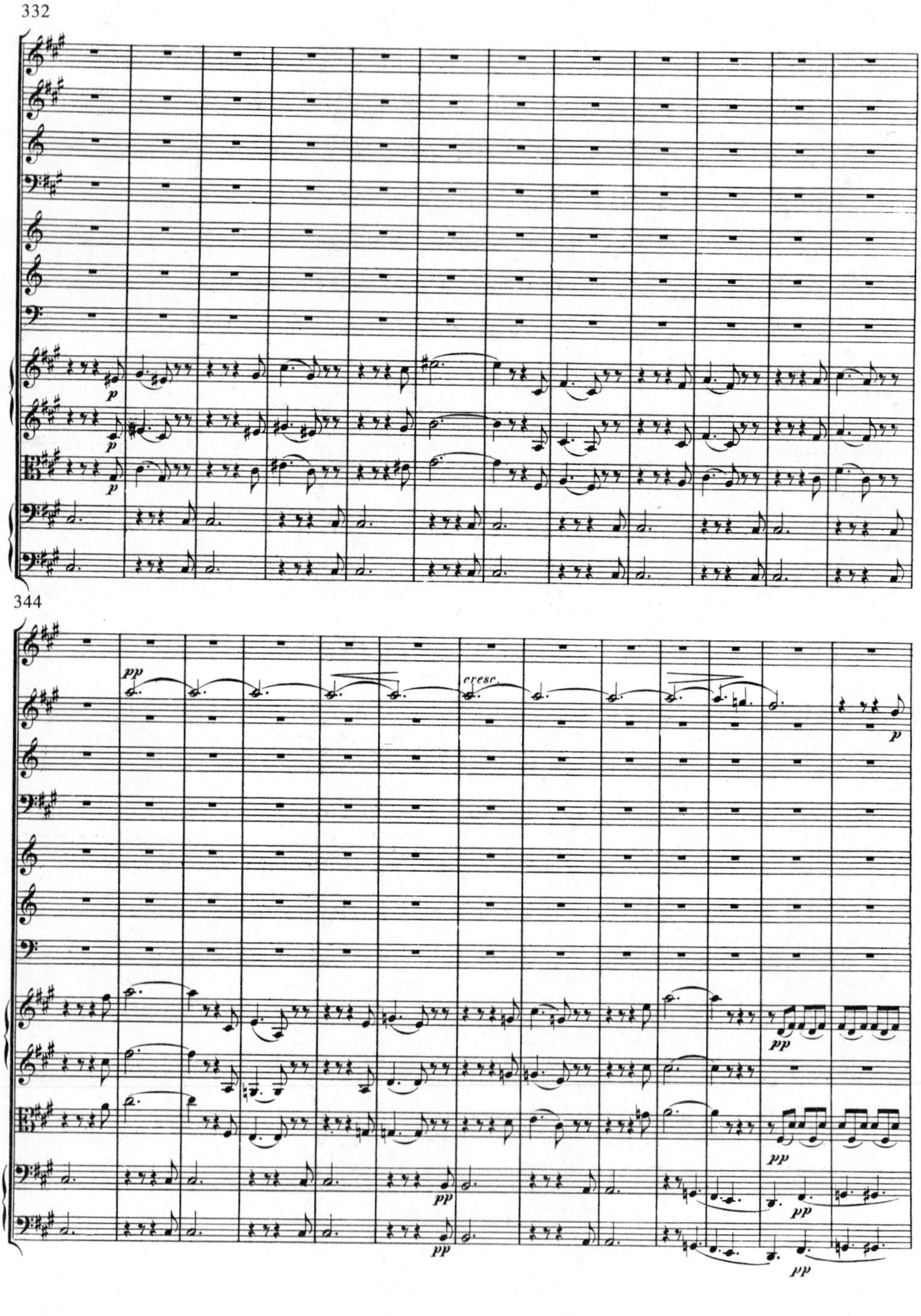
332
344
cresc.

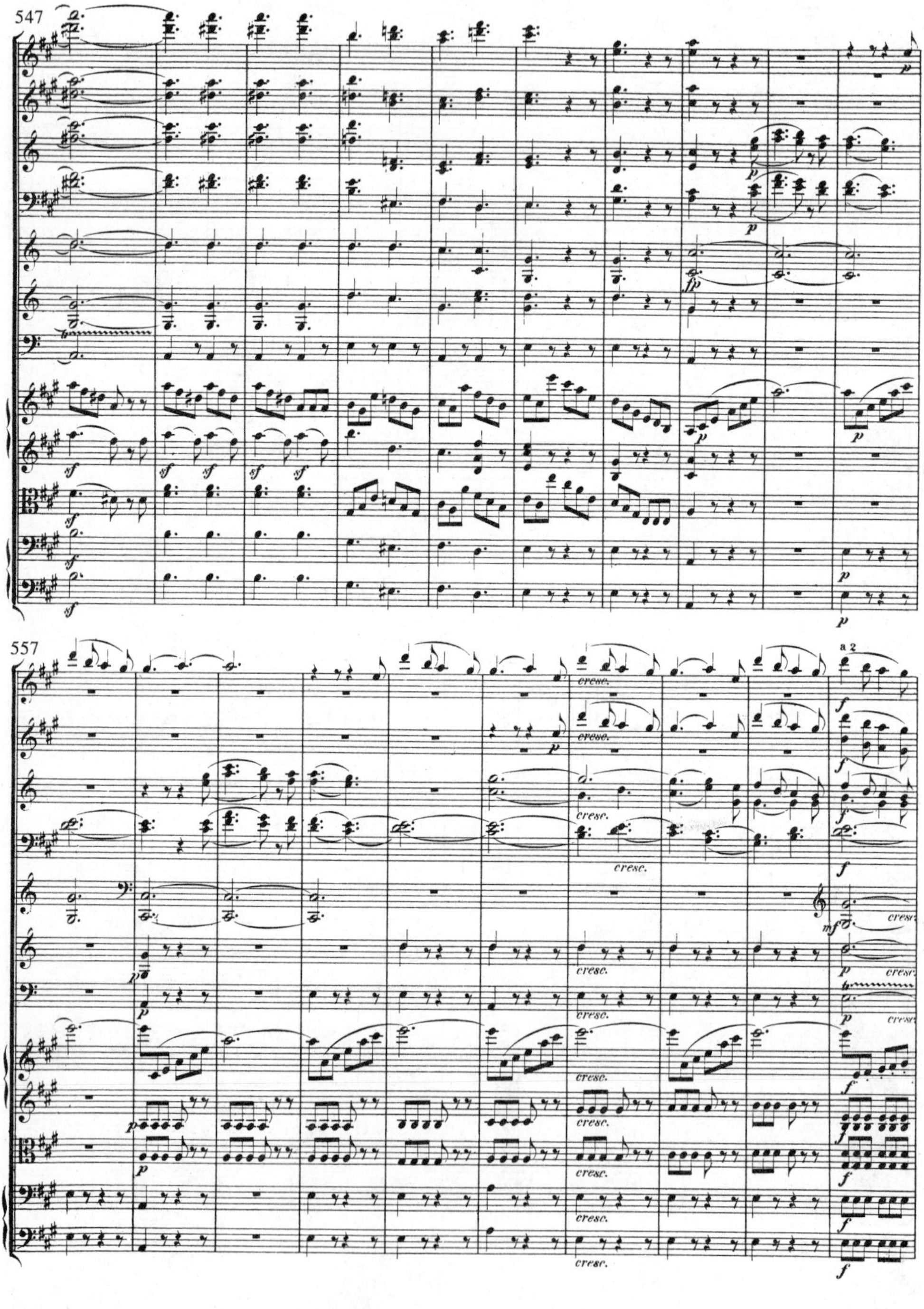
547
557
cresc.
a 2

II

95

III

Con moto moderato

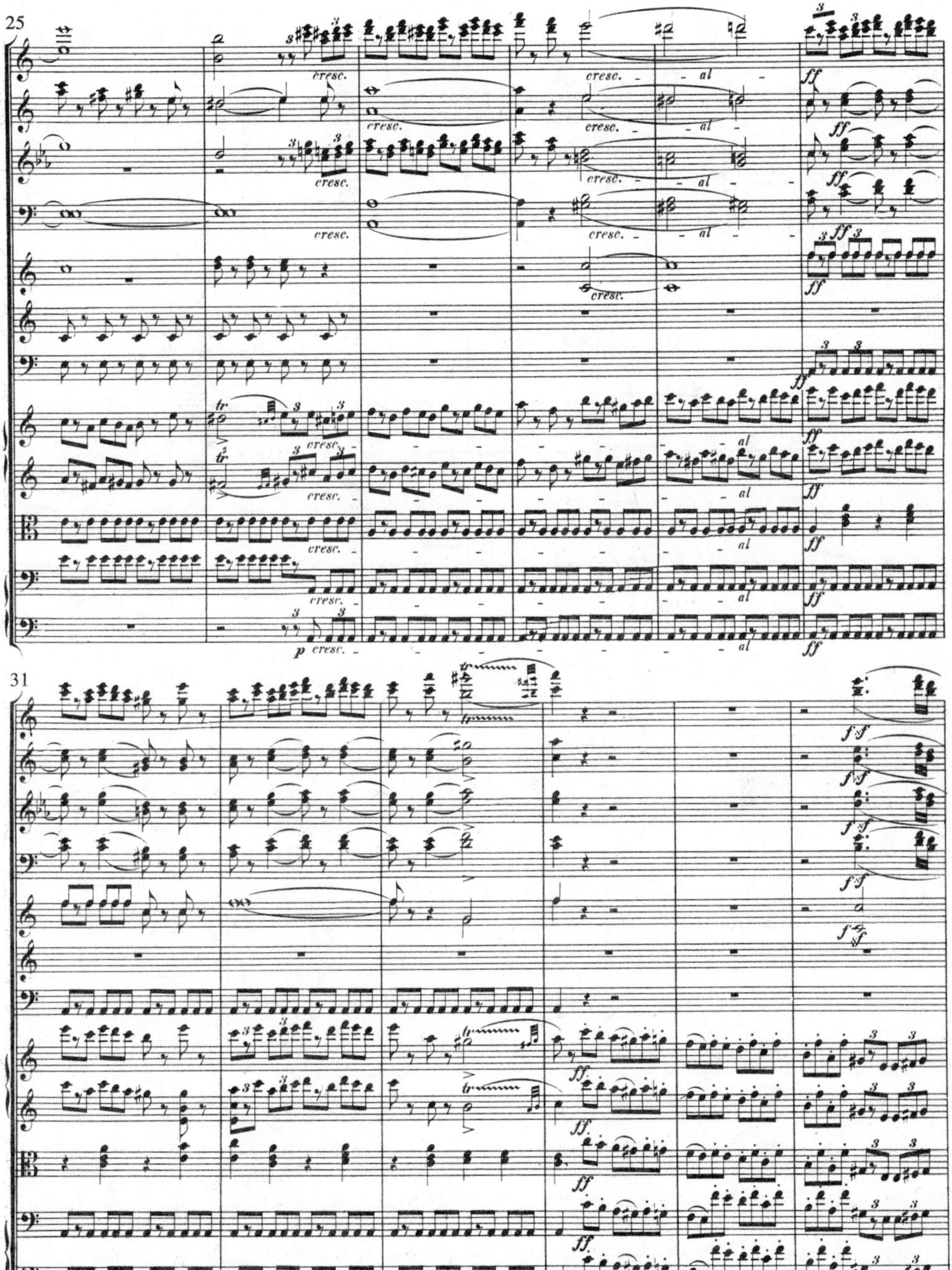
25
cresc.
al
ff
tr
p
31
f

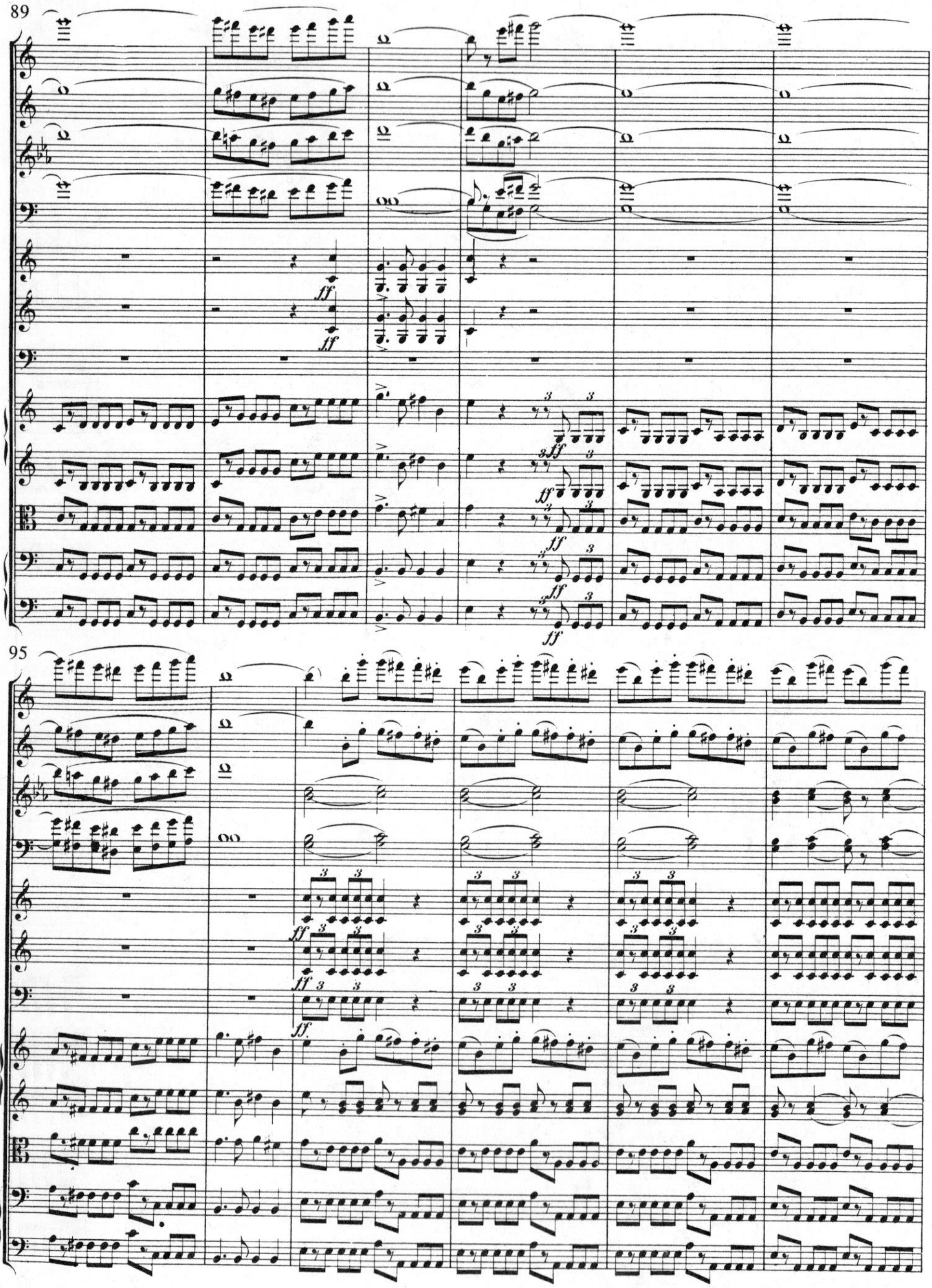
89
ff
95
ff

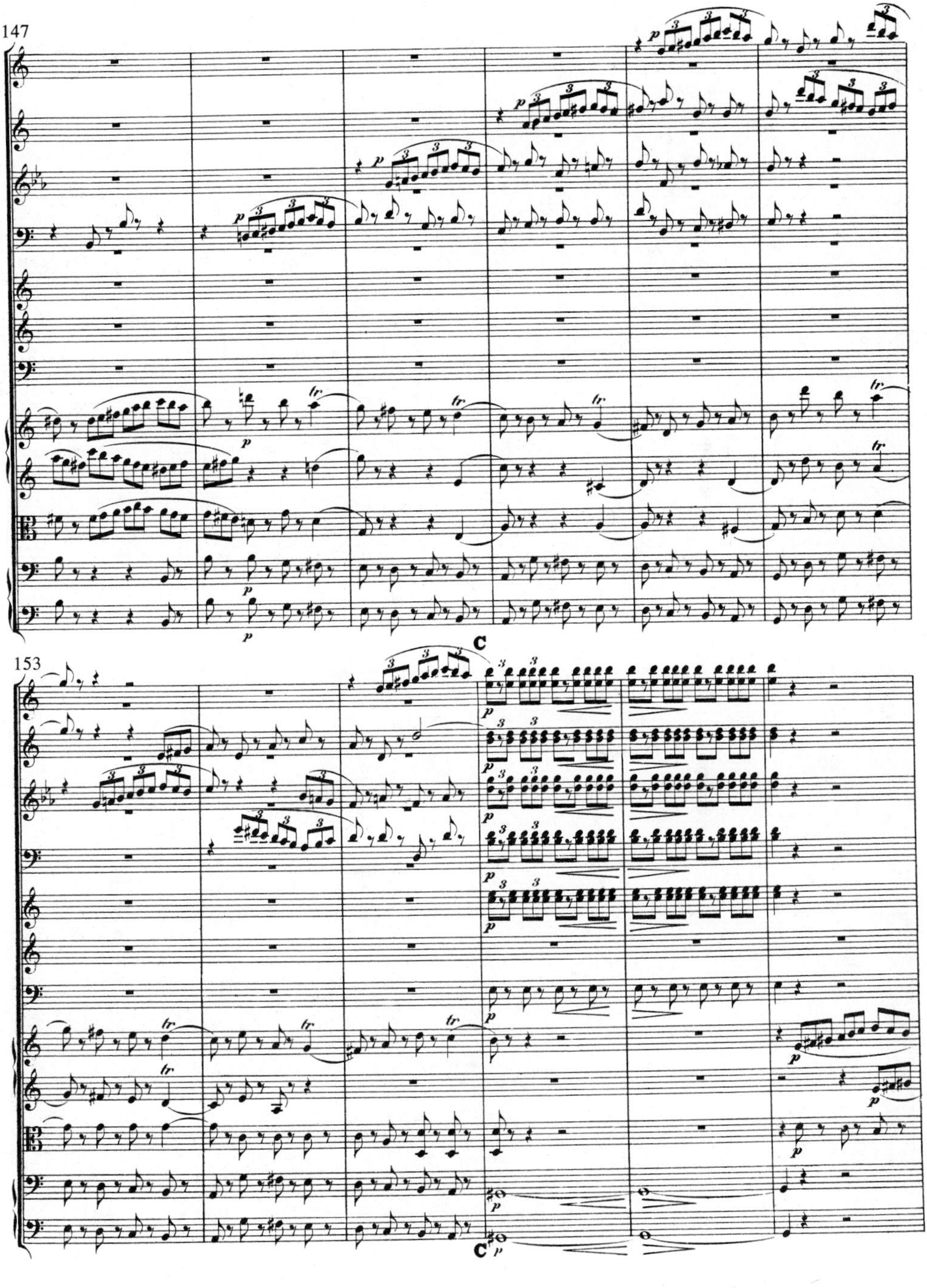
147
153
C
p
tr
3

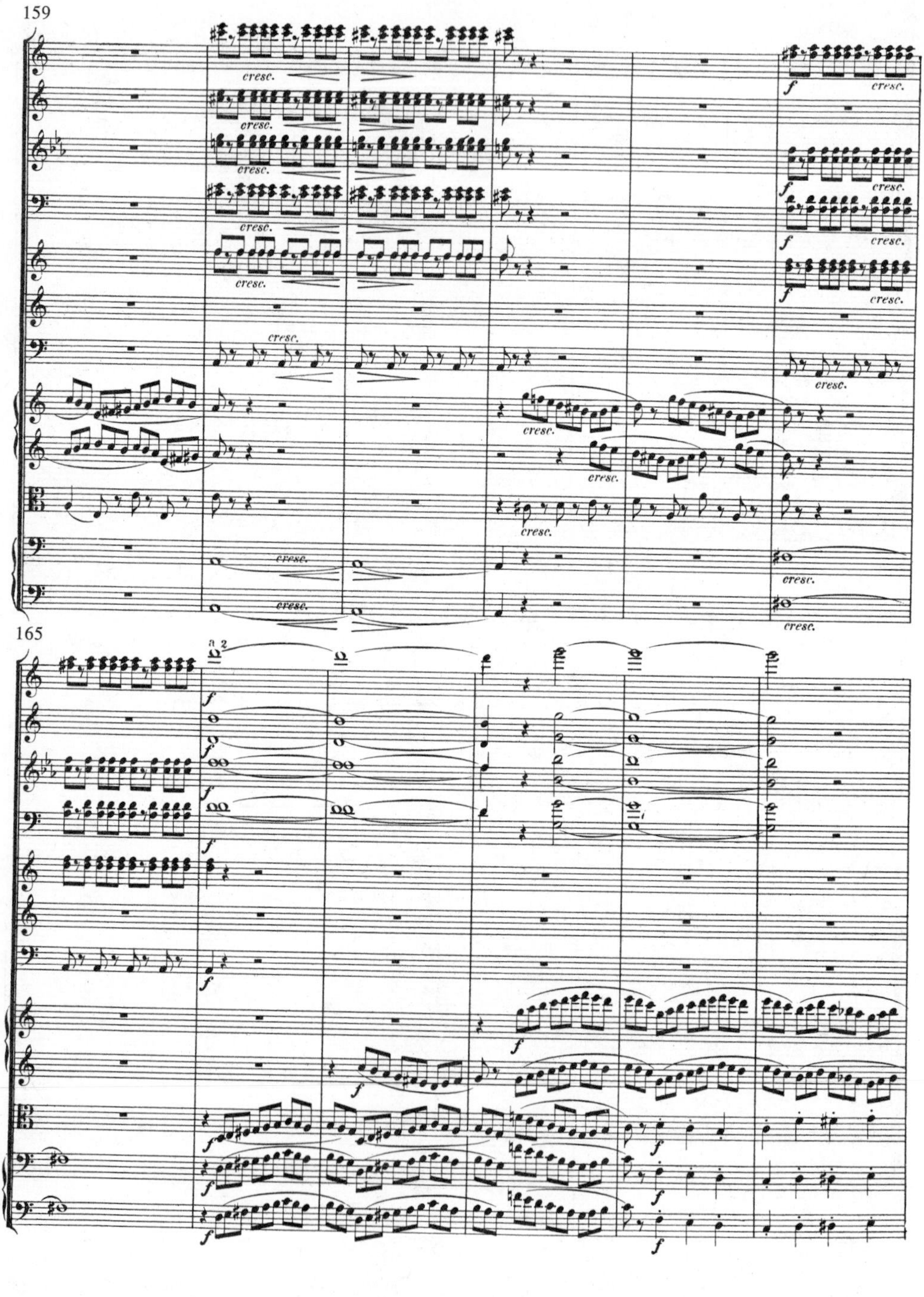
159
cresc.
f
165
a 2

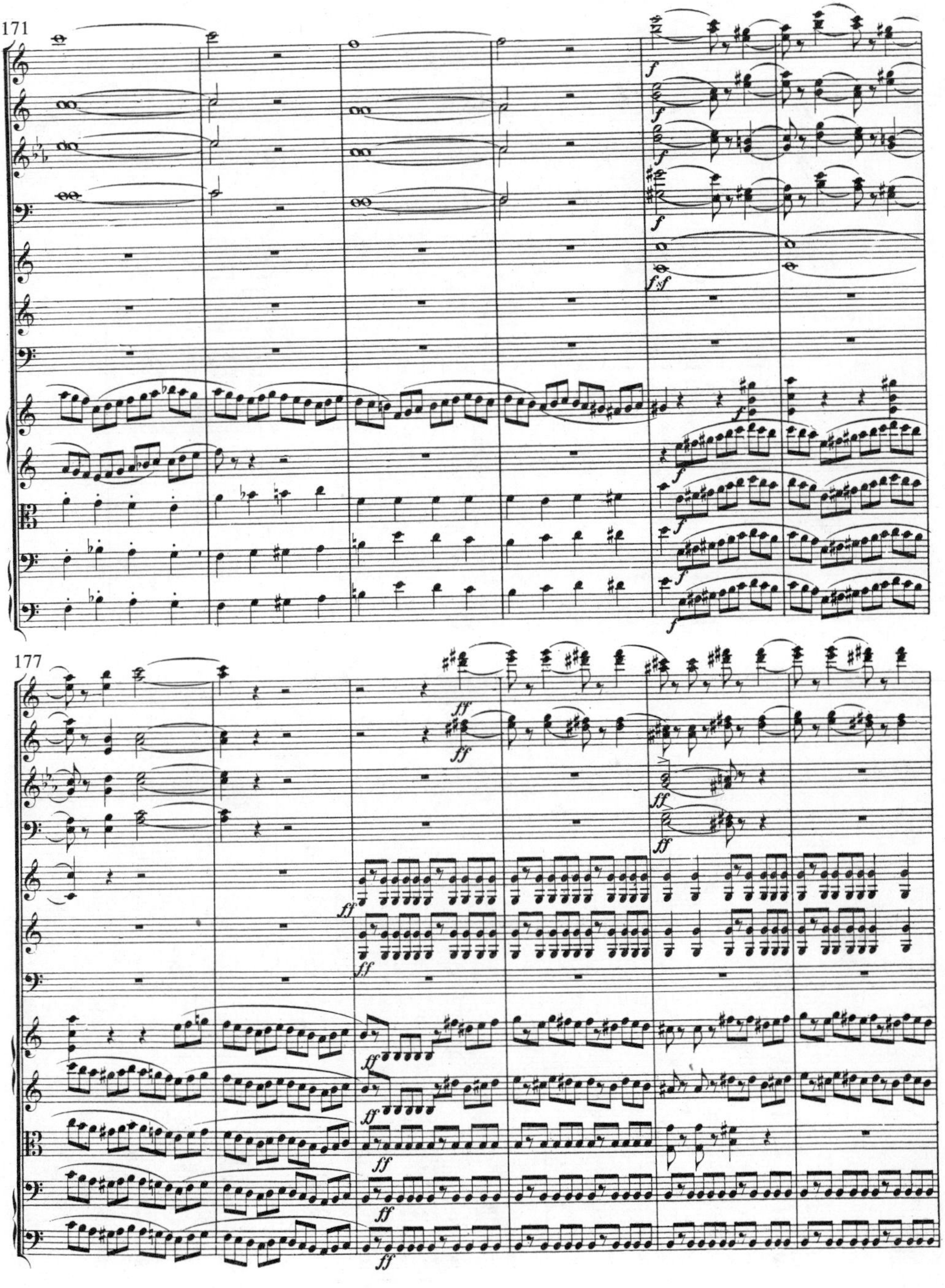
171
f
177
ff

183
ff
ff
ff
ff
ff
ff
ff
ff
ff
189
ff
ff
ff
a 2.
ff
ff
ff
D
f
f
f
p
dim.
dim.
p
p
p
p
D
fp

Robert Schumann *(1810–1856)*

SYMPHONY NO. 4 IN D MINOR, OP. 120

(1841, revised 1851)

INSTRUMENTATION

2 Flutes *(Fl.)*
2 Oboes *(Ob.)*
2 Clarinets in B♭ *(Clar. in B)*
2 Bassoons *(Fag.)*

4 Horns *(Cor.)* in F, D
2 Trumpets *(Tr.)* in F, E
3 Trombones *(Trboni.)*

Timpani *(Timp.)*

Violin I
Violin II
Viola
Cello *(Vcl.)*
Double Bass *(Basso)*

SCHERZO.

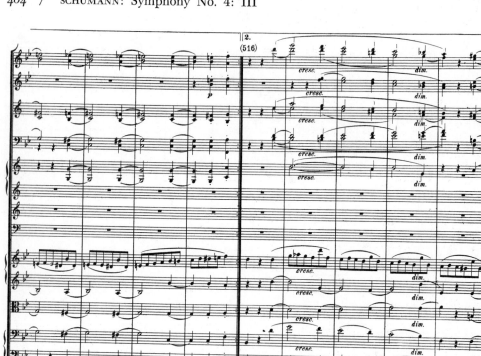

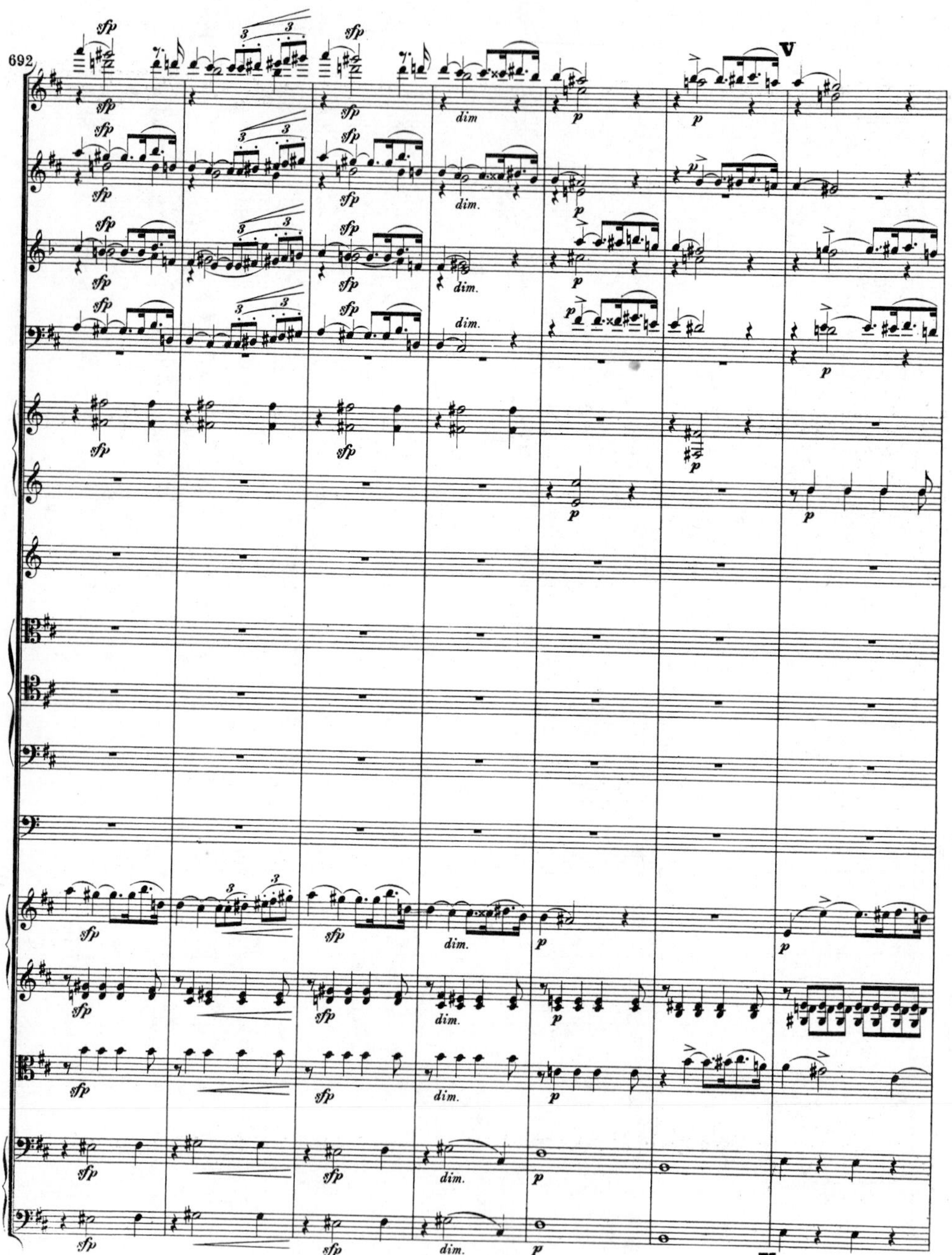
692
sfp
dim
p
dim.

Peter Ilyich Tchaikovsky (1840–1893)

SYMPHONY NO. 4 IN F MINOR, OP. 36

(1877)

INSTRUMENTATION

1 Piccolo *(Kl. Fl.)*
2 Flutes *(Fl.)*
2 Oboes *(Ob.)*
2 Clarinets *(Klar.)* in B♭ *(B)*, A
2 Bassoons *(Fag.)*

4 Horns *(Hrn.)* in F
2 Trumpets *(Trp.)* in F
3 Trombones *(Pos.)*
Bass Tuba *(Btb.)*

Timpani *(Pk.)*
Triangle *(Triang.)*
Cymbals *(Beck.)*
Bass Drum *(Gr. Tr.)*

Violin I *(Viol. 1)*
Violin II *(Viol. 2)*
Viola *(Vla.)*
Violoncello *(Vc.)*
Double Bass *(Kb.)*

I

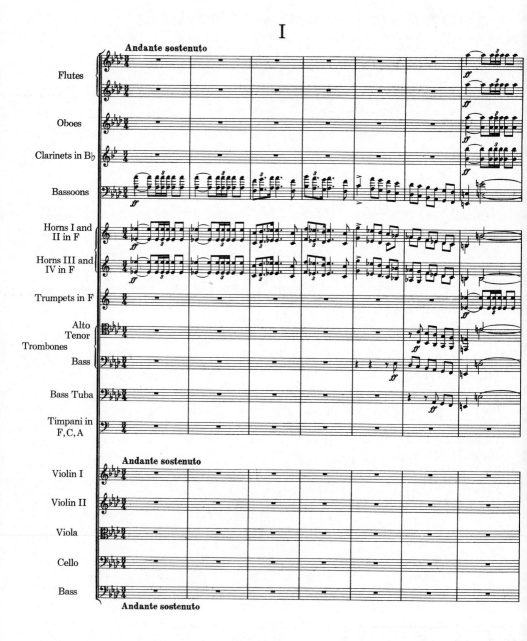

100
E
1.
Fl.
2.
Ob.1.2
Klar.
1.2 in B
mf dolce grazioso
a 2
Fag.1.2
mf dolce
1.2.in F
Hrn.
3.4.in F
Trp.1.2
in F
A.T.
Pos.
B.
Btb.
muta C in H, A in Fis
Pk.
E
Viol.1
p
Viol.2
p
Vla.
p
Vc.
p
Kb.
p
E

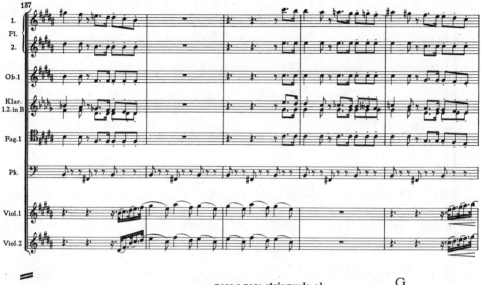

192
Klar. 1.2 in B
Fag. 1.2
1.2. in F
Hrn.
3.4. in F
Trp. 1.2 in F
Pk.
Viol. 1
Viol. 2
Vla.
Vc.
Kb.
a 2
fff con tutta forza
199
L
1. Fl. 2.
B.-Pos.
Btb.
muta H in C, Fis in A

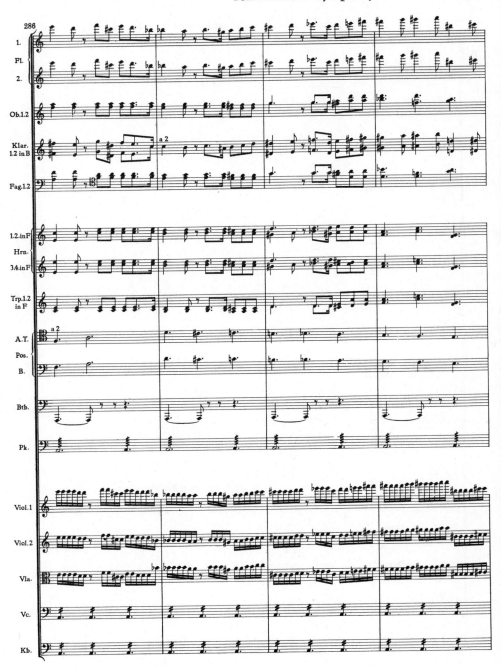

II

III. Scherzo: Pizzicato ostinato

378
Kl. Fl.
1.
Fl.
2.
Ob. 1.2
Klar. 1,2 in A
Fag. 1.2
1.2 in F
Hrn
3.4 in F
Viol. 1
Viol. 2
Vla.
Vc.
Kb.
a 2
cresc.
ff
388
Hrn.

IV. Finale

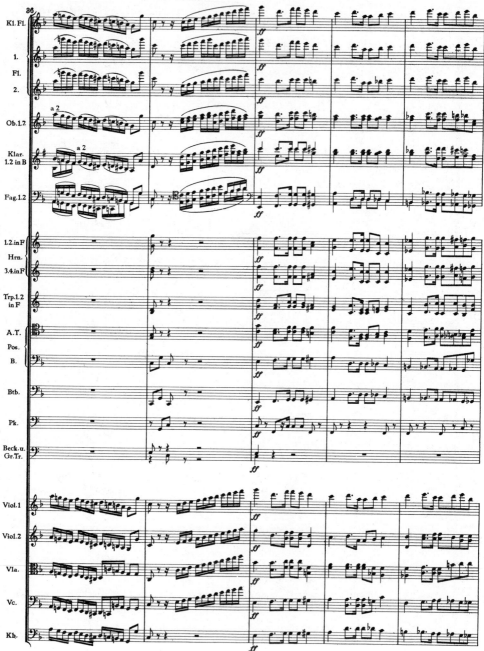

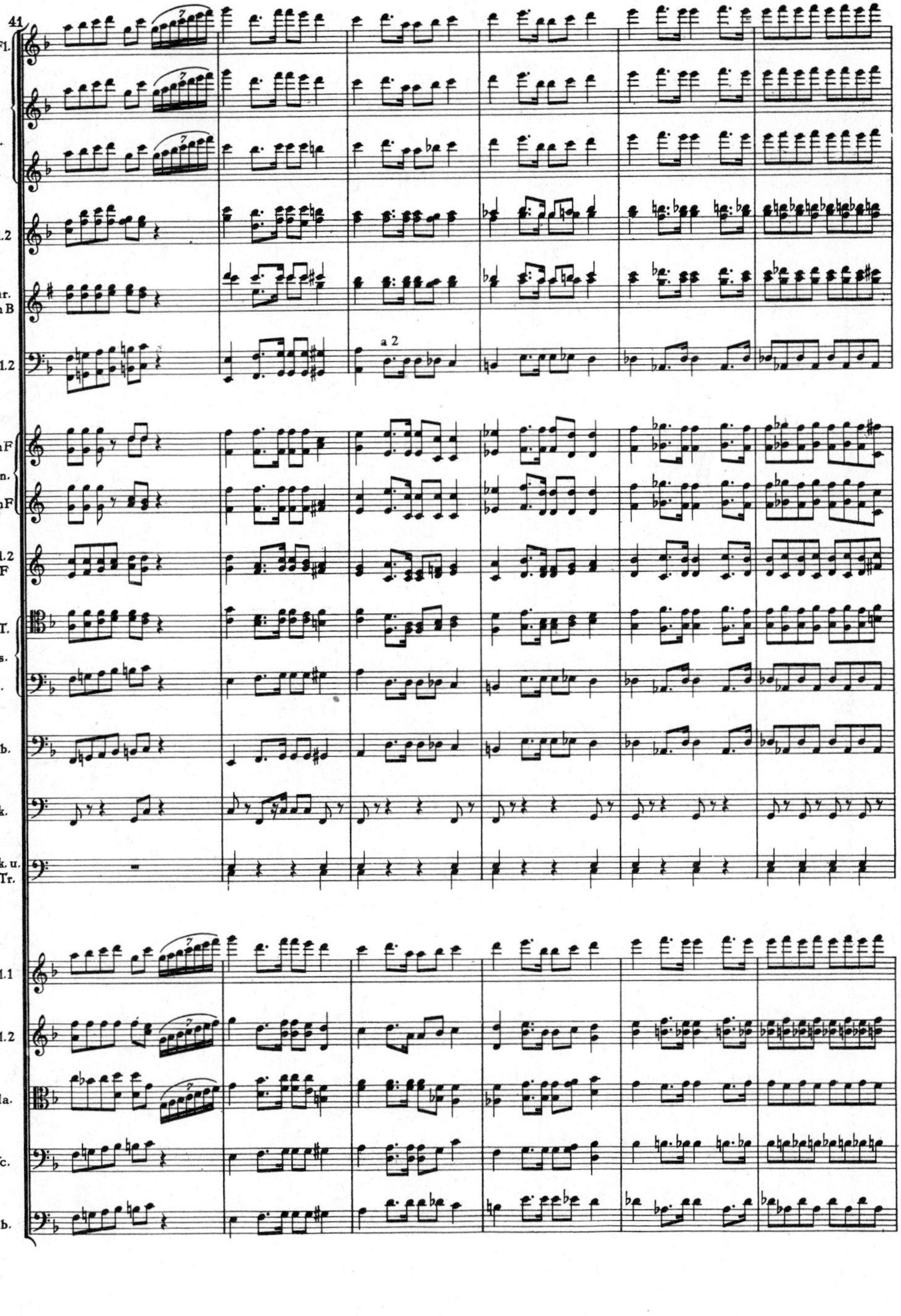
41
Kl. Fl.
1.
Fl.
2.
Ob. 1.2
Klar. 1.2 in B
Fag. 1.2
a 2
1.2. in F
Hrn.
3.4. in F
Trp. 1.2 in F
A. T.
Pos.
B.
Btb.
Pk.
Beck. u. Gr. Tr.
Viol. 1
Viol. 2
Vla.
Vc.
Kb.

272
Kl. Fl.
1.
Fl.
2.
Ob. 1.2
Klar. 1.2 in B
Fag. 1.2
1.2. in F
Hrn.
3.4. in F
Trp. 1.2 in F
a 2
A.T.
Pos.
B.
Btb.
Pk.
Triang.
Beck. u. Gr. Tr.
8
Viol. 1
Viol. 2
Vla.
Vc.
Kb.

277
Kl. Fl.
1.
Fl.
2.
Ob. 1.2
Klar. 1.2 in B
a 2
Fag. 1.2
a 2
1.2. in F
Hrn.
3.4. in F
Trp. 1.2 in F
A. T.
Pos.
B.
Btb.
Pk.
Triang.
Beck. u. Gr. Tr.
Viol. 1
Viol. 2
Vla.
Vc.
Kb.

287
Kl. Fl.
1.
Fl.
2.
Ob.1.2
Klar. 1.2 in B
Fag.1.2
1.2.in F
Hrn.
3.4.in F
Trp.1.2 in F
A. T.
Pos.
B.
Btb.
Pk.
Triang.
Beck.u. Gr.Tr.
Viol.1
Viol.2
Vla.
Vc.
Kb.

Johannes Brahms (1833–1897)

SYMPHONY NO. 3 IN F MAJOR, OP. 90

(1 8 8 3)

INSTRUMENTATION

2 Flutes *(Fl.)*
2 Oboes *(Ob.)*
2 Clarinets *(Klar.)* in B♭ *(B)*, A
2 Bassoons *(Fag.)*
Contrabassoon *(K.-Fag.)*

4 Horns *(Hr.)* in C, F
2 Trumpets *(Trpt.)* in F
3 Trombones *(Pos.)*

Timpani *(Pk.)*

Violin I *(1. Viol.)*
Violin II *(2. Viol.)*
Viola *(Br.)*
Cello *(Vcl.)*
Double Bass *(K.-B.)*

I

III

IV

Anton Bruckner (1824–1896)

ADAGIO *FROM* SYMPHONY NO. 7

IN E MAJOR

(1883)

INSTRUMENTATION

2 Flutes *(Fl.)*
2 Oboes *(Ob.)*
2 Clarinets *(Cl.)* in A
2 Bassoons *(Fag.)*

4 Horns *(Hr.)* in F
3 Trumpets *(Tr.)* in F
3 Trombones *(Pos.)*
2 Tenor Tubas *(Tub. I & II)* in B♭
2 Bass Tubas *(Tub. III & IV)* in F
Contrabass Tuba *(C. B. Tub.)*

Timpani *(Pk.)* in C, G
Triangle *(Triang.)*
Cymbals *(Becken)*

Violin I *(Viol. I)*
Violin II *(Viol. II)*
Viola
Cello
Double Bass

Antonín Dvořák *(1841–1904)*

SYMPHONY NO. 8 IN G MAJOR, OP. 88

(OLD NO. 4)

(1889)

INSTRUMENTATION

2 Flutes *(Flauti)*
II doubles on Piccolo
2 Oboes *(Oboi)*
2 Clarinets *(Clarinetti)* in A, B♭
2 Bassoons *(Fagotti)*

4 Horns *(Corni)* in F, C, D
2 Trumpets *(Trombe)* in F, C, D
3 Trombones *(Tromboni)*
Tuba

Timpani

Violin I *(Violino I)*
Violin II *(Violino II)*
Viola
Cello
Double Bass *(Contra-Basso)*

I

86

191

199

221

226

257

261

269

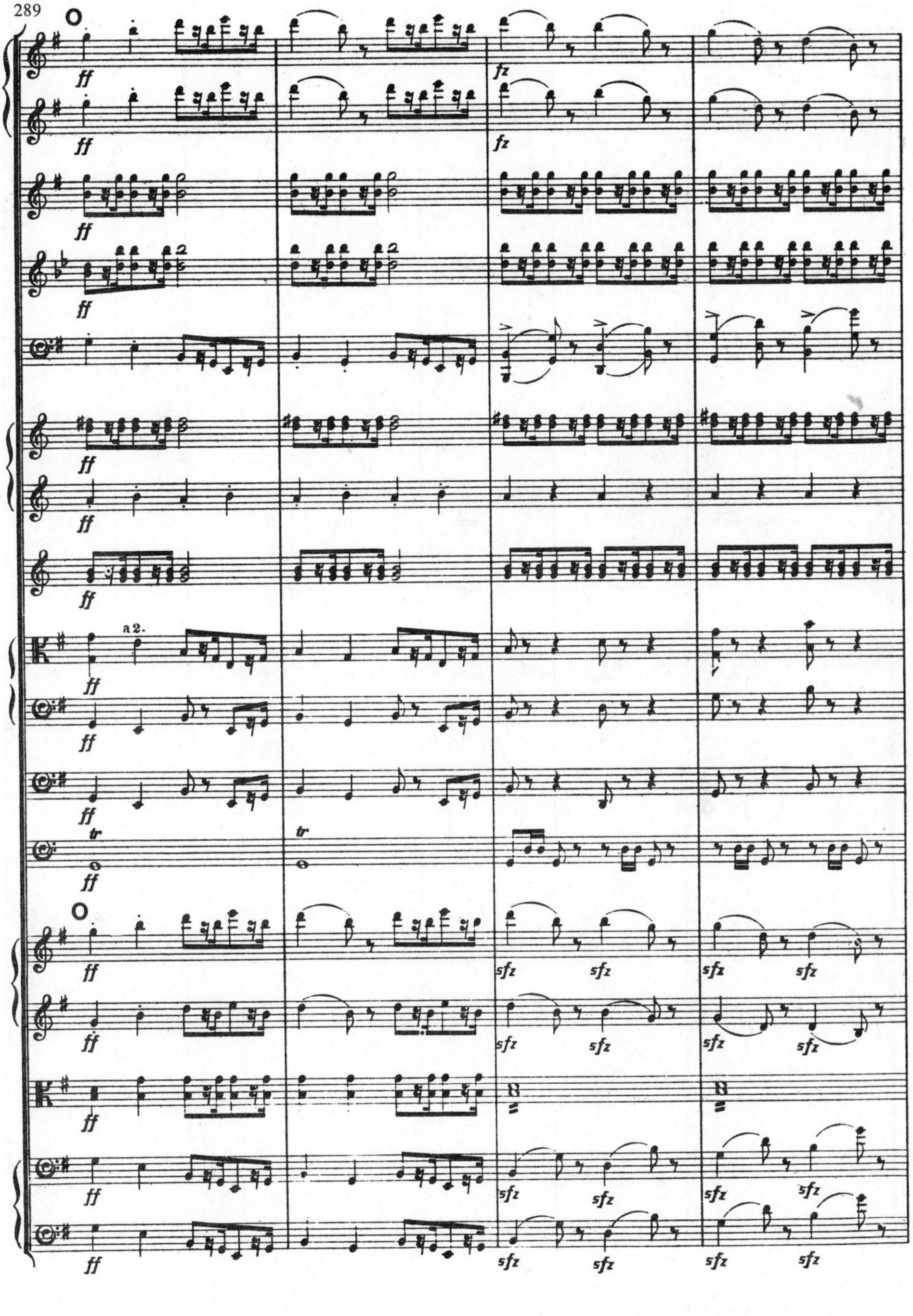
289
O
ff
fz
a 2.
tr
O
sfz

293

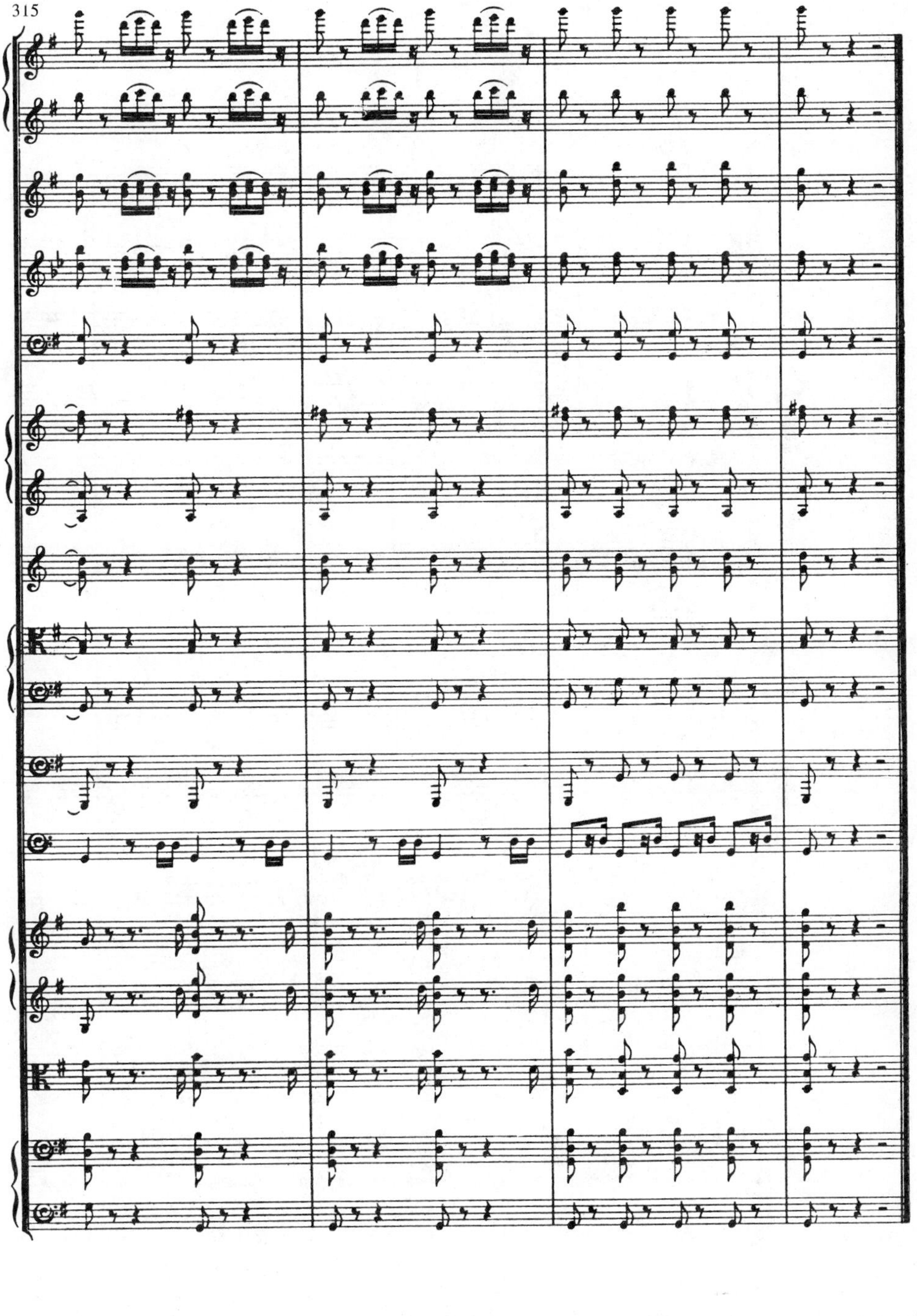
315

II

46

55

D

pp

p

pp

pp

pp

mf

Violin Solo.

espressivo

ppp

pizz.

pp

D

62

90

106

138

147

III

31

72

109

126

141

158

CODA.

189

IV

34

51

119

144

184

207

237

276

303

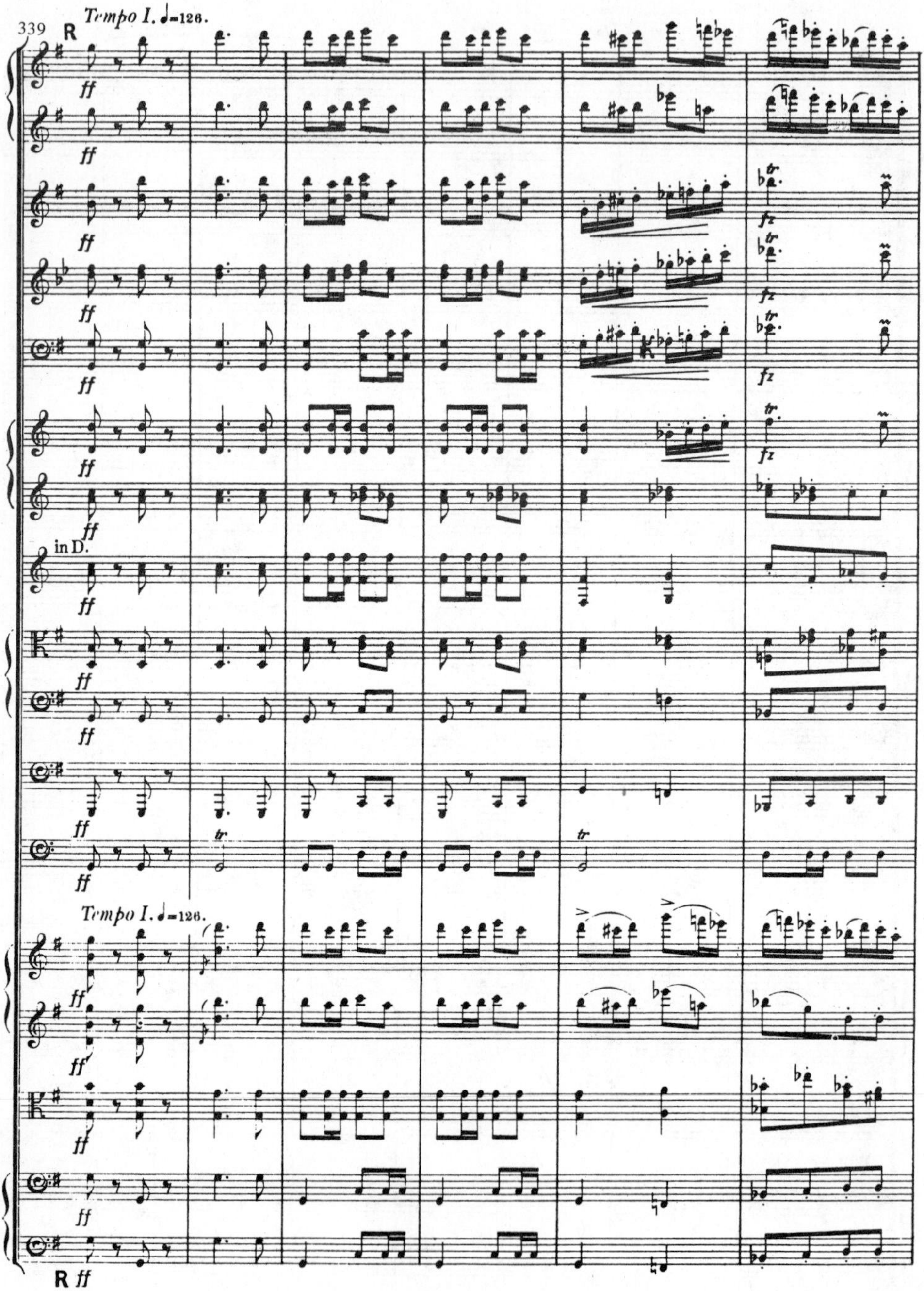
339
R
Tempo I. ♩=126.
ff
in D.
tr
fz
Tempo I. ♩=126.
R ff

345

370

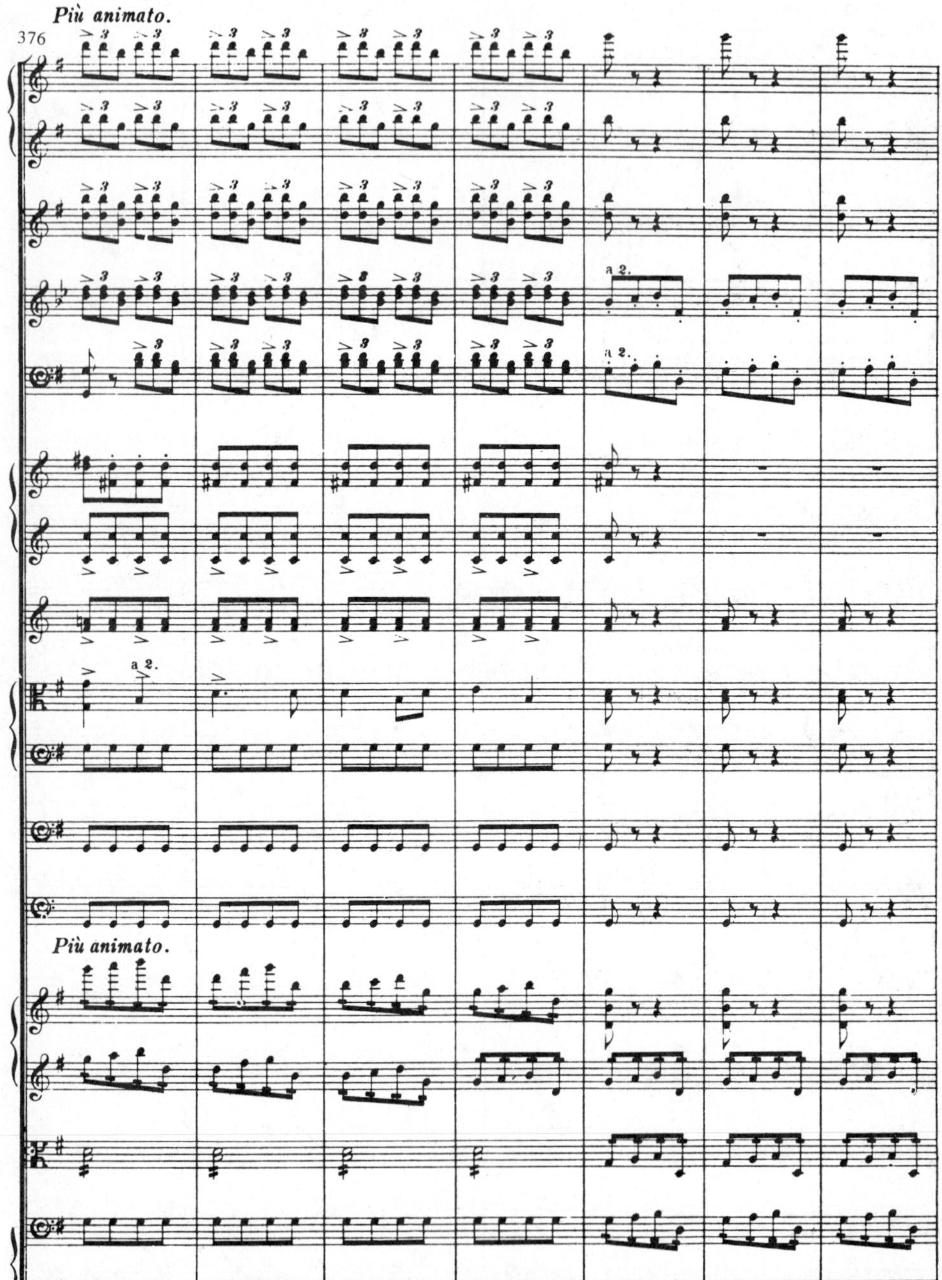
Più animato.
376
3
a 2.
Più animato.

Appendix

Reading an Orchestral Score

CLEFS

The music for some instruments is written in clefs other than the familiar treble and bass. In the following example, middle C is shown in the four clefs used in orchestral scores:

Treble   *Alto*   *Tenor*   *Bass*
clef   *clef*   *clef*   *clef*

The *alto clef* is primarily used in viola parts. The *tenor clef* is employed for cello, bassoon, and trombone parts when these instruments play in a high register.

TRANSPOSING INSTRUMENTS

The music for some instruments is customarily written at a pitch different from their actual sound. The following list, with examples, shows the main transposing instruments and the degree of transposition.

Instrument	*Transposition*	*Written Note*	*Actual Sound*
Piccolo, Celesta	sound an octave higher than written		
Trumpet in F	sound a fourth higher than written		
Trumpet in E	sound a major third higher than written		

Instrument	*Transposition*	*Written Note* *Actual Sound*

Clarinet in E♭,
    Trumpet in E♭
	sound a minor third
	    higher than written	

Trumpet in D	sound a major second higher than written	

Clarinet in B♭,
    Trumpet in B♭,
    Cornet in B♭
	sound a major second
	    lower than written	

Clarinet in A,
    Horn in A
    Cornet in A
	sound a minor third
	    lower than written	

English horn,
    Horn in F
	sound a fifth
	    lower than written	

Horn in E	sound a minor sixth lower than written	
Horn in E♭	sound a minor sixth lower than written	
Horn in D	sound a major seventh lower than written	

Horn in C,
    Double bass
	sound an octave
	    lower than written	

Tenor Tuba in B♭	sound a major ninth lower than written	
Bass Tuba in F	sound a perfect twelfth lower than written	

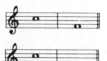

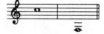